Index

First Edition printed in 2004
ISBN 978-981-05-7546-5

Front cover & layout designed by Graphicat Design Place, Singapore

IMPORTANT NOTE

This book was prepared by Steve Douglas,
Managing Director of Australasian Taxation Services Pty Ltd (ATS).

ATS is a Registered Tax Agent in Australia and has been advising Australian expatriates since 1995 and helping them set manageable strategies to achieve the best results.

We hope this general guide gives you some direction and we always remain available to assist you further.

The information in this book is intended as a guide to the aspects of Australian taxation that need to be considered by Australian expatriates. You will also need to address the Taxation issues in the country of employment.

No person should act solely on the information contained herein, as the complexities of Australian Taxation Legislation would require due analysis of each individual's circumstances prior to any decision.

1. About The Author

Steve Douglas is the co founder and Managing Director of Australasian Taxation Services (ATS), and Chairman of the SMATS Group.

ATS was established in 1995 to provide specialist taxation services to property investors throughout Southeast Asia and today attend to the Australian taxation needs of thousands of property investors based all around the world.

His areas of specialisation include the Australian taxation aspects of property investment and expatriate and migration taxation planning.

ATS has delivered many presentations on Australian property taxation matters in Singapore, Hong Kong, Malaysia, China, United Kingdom, Dubai, USA, Taiwan, Vietnam and Australia on behalf of industry organizations and developers, including the Real Estate Institute of Western Australia and various Australian Chamber of Commerce's, focusing on how investors can benefit from the taxation laws relating to property investment, the impact of GST on property and the impact of CGT changes to the property investor.

He also consults and presents on the specific tax planning issues for Australian Expatriates and intended Australian migrants.

Steve's seminar presentations have attracted over 10,000 attendees, educating them on the key financial and taxation aspects of investing in Australian property.

SMATS Group encompasses the Taxation business operations as well as Specialist Mortgage, the leading independent Finance Broker to offshore-based Australian property investors and Expatriates.

In 2005, Steve launched his property information portal, *www.aussieproperty.com* which has grown to become the benchmark in online information, financial tools and specialised resources for the Australian property investor based abroad, welcoming over 3,000 unique visitors a week.

An avid researcher and commentator on the Australian property market,

Steve has also been featured in articles by South China Morning Post, Singapore Business Times, Australian Entrepreneur Magazine, Benchmark, Western Australia Property & Investment, International Property Magazine and Property Link.

Steve began his career with Ernst & Young in 1984 and established a private taxation practise in 1988 specialising in small business taxation and management.

He is a Fellow of the Taxation Institute of Australia and a Registered Tax Agent.

2. Foreword

I had the great fortune of meeting Steve Douglas at a mate's farewell party at the Australian High Commissioner's residence in Singapore in 1999.

I had recently married and my wife Kathy was slightly bemused at the tardy state of my taxation affairs that I had left behind in Australia some six years earlier. Nothing too serious, mind you, just several years of non-filing of the annual tax return since I had left Oz for the expatriate life of Southeast Asia.

Kathy announced to me at the party that she had just met a fellow that I should meet, on the basis that he was an Australian tax specialist based in Singapore and Perth, and that I seriously needed to get my tax matters in order.

Always keen to meet someone new, I grabbed a couple of cold Tigers and introduced myself, handing one to Steve. It turned out to be the most financially beneficial meeting of my life.

Steve asked me about myself, and I explained in a slightly embarrassed manner that I had been a bit slack in lodging my returns since arriving in Singapore.

In a very reassuring tone Steve said to me that he could get it sorted out as long as I had kept all of my relevant documents. "Just put it all in a box and drop it around on Monday and we'll take it from there. Now, what are you doing with all of this money you've been earning?"

On this question I was on much steadier ground. "Paying the house in Sydney off, mate," I proudly stated, "I think I've knocked about fifty grand off the mortgage in three years!"

"Well mate," Steve said in a grave tone, "I think we might have to have a look at that. Have you ever heard of Australian tax credits?"

"Oh yeah..." I lied in a not too convincing tone. "...ahhm, that's when....ahmm..." Steve recognized the response and saved me further embarrassment by jumping in. "Don't worry, I'll explain it to you after I have a look at your records. Now, how about another beer?"

The next Monday I met with Steve in his office and he told me that I was making a big financial mistake in paying off my house. "Get a loan, and go shopping for another one" was his advice. "The Australian tax laws represents a once in a life time opportunity for Aussies living overseas," Steve explained, "and the longer that you are away, the better off you will be when you get back, if you take the initiative now".

We followed Steve's advice and bought a flat in Melbourne within two months. A year later we bought another, and then a third investment property. The capital value of these investments has increased some forty percent since, and our financial future is extremely secure.

In fact, we feel so comfortable with our portfolio that I have left a full expatriate position in Singapore to fulfil a lifetime dream – running my own training business with my wife.

Bernie Jones
Singapore

3. Introduction

Welcome to one of the fastest growing groups in the world, the Australian Expatriate.

There is now almost a million of us walking the globe somewhere, making an impact in economics, business, environment, sports, culture and entertainment.

It seems that wherever you are, you can always hear a friendly "G'day".

When I wrote the first edition of this book, it was my first attempt at writing a full-length effort and I did it with great eagerness and excitement.

With over 2,000 books sold on the original print, it surpassed my expectations, and now I present the 2nd Edition, with just as much excitement as the first.

It has been particularly pleasing to discover from many that they have found the book through a wide variety of means and that it circulates Expat communities throughout the world.

Of more importance to me is the fact that people keep thanking me for the effort in writing the book and the positive contribution it has made to them. This is my driving motivation.

Based on the feedback received I have added and modified various areas, but kept true to the original theme.

That is to educate and enhance the opportunities of all the Australian Expat's wherever they may be, and allow them to maximise their time abroad.

Many Australians working abroad do not fully comprehend the taxation planning advantages available to them whilst overseas.

In many cases people return to Australia financially better off through savings built up, but have failed to maximise their time overseas by not planning for taxation benefits that can be easily accumulated through safe and prudent property investment.

This book serves as a guide to the Australian Expatriate to help you through the tax laws and allow you to return to Australia at a future date with substantial accrued tax credits that can significantly reduce the Income Tax on salary or retirement incomes and may even allow a number of years of tax free status.

Many expatriates are lured by "Tax Free Schemes" and international savings plans whilst overseas. These are often expensive and confusing, and most importantly, DO NOT protect against Australian tax when you return to Australia.

This book will help identify the ways you can achieve significant tax benefits legally, with a minimum of risk and expense, whilst at the same time prudently building your wealth and savings and presenting opportunities to acquire property that may not have been affordable during the time you lived in Australia.

Please excuse me for using plain English and no Tax Jargon, I wanted to keep you awake!

4. Welcome Aboard

There are different reasons why we become expatriates but at the end of the day there is always a common thread, that we are trying to improve our lives, particularly financially.

Most expatriates would be earning more than when they were in Australia, and most likely be paying less income tax. As such our disposable income increases and hopefully most of that flows towards savings.

It is very common in the first few years of being an expatriate that you will spend a lot of this additional disposable income rewarding yourself with all the things that you wanted but could not previously afford, but eventually you will have to take stock and start thinking of what is best for you long term.

Respect this time of your life and it will reward you forever, otherwise you will long regret this lost opportunity.

Even for those that do not think they are that well off financially in their position, and may have come overseas to advance the technical aspects of their careers, the opportunities are just as profound.

The combination of similar or greater earnings, lower taxation and the capacity to be a landlord and generate rental income, all combine to ensure we can achieve results beyond our normal expectations.

Obviously, the more you earn the more impact you can potentially make which but anyone can achieve. It just takes a personal commitment and a small amount of dedication.

For a moment, cast your mind back to when you were in Australia earning a salary.

By the time tax has been paid, the mortgage, school fees, general living and cost of kids has gone, we all remember how little was left over.

Now imagine being back in Australia without a home mortgage and with no tax to pay. What a life that would be.

Well that is what can happen if you take advantage of this special time abroad.

Aside from all the personal benefits that you will experience as an Expatriate, the ability to return to Australia financially secure, own your home and reduce the impact of taxation on your life, is now in your hands.

It is well known that knowledge is power.

This book will give you the knowledge you need, you make the decisions as to how powerful this knowledge can become.

5. Don't Swim Against The Tide

Australia has a very poor reputation when it comes to personal income tax.

It is true that if you are a salary earner in Australia, trying to bring up a family and live a normal life, it is extremely hard to get ahead and build up any savings.

Great changes are happening in Australia as the personal tax rates are improving almost on a yearly basis.

When I wrote the first edition in 2004, the top tax rate in Australia was 47% once your income exceeded A$62,500 p.a.

The Howard Government has aggressively tackled these rates and as I write this edition not more that two years later in the 2007 Financial Year, the top rate has reduced to 45% and comes into effect once taxable income exceeds A$150,000 p.a.

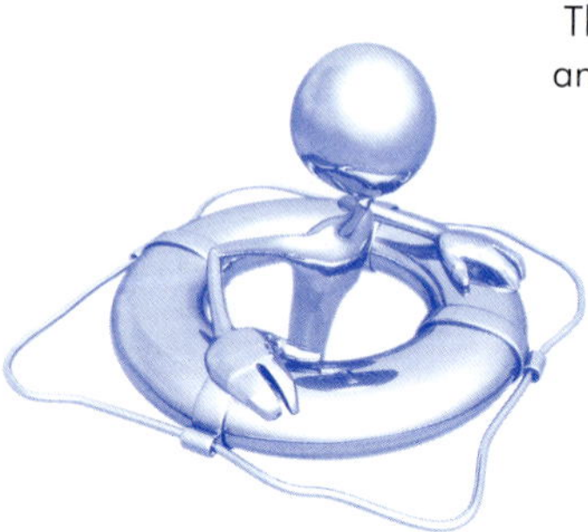

This is a significant change in a very short time and a trend I believe will continue in the future.

One key reason for this is the desire to lure expatriates, such as you, back to Australia, using the tax rate reductions as the carrot.

Nonetheless for those living in Australia these tax rates are welcomed but may not necessarily lead to improved savings ability, perhaps just a more enjoyable lifestyle.

For most Australians, the Tax Free status of the family home is still their only chance to build up wealth. Sadly most people do not fully realise that your home is not a true asset, as we tend to sell and "upgrade" when the value increases.

All that aside, the Australian taxation system is actually very investor friendly, particularly when you follow a sensible and government encouraged path.

To me it is like a fast flowing river, swimming against it will only exhaust you and you will hardly make any progress. However if you swim with the tide, your energy is saved, the distance you travel is far greater and the tide has done much of the work to get you there.

As such I have spent my career finding ways to swim with the Australian taxation system and have steered clear of gimmicky tax schemes that were obviously dangerous from a tax and investment perspective.

What I have found is that with forward planning and safe investment principles based around Australian property not only is the journey easy, it is safe and incredibly rewarding.

The Australian taxation system supports real investment, offering substantial reductions in tax when funds are kept active in the system in areas that the government acknowledges as valuable, such as property and Australian equity markets.

By using the options legally available to you the results can be far more successful than trying to scam.

This is clearly evident when you realise that generating capital gains rather than income greatly reduces the tax burden as only half of gains on assets held longer than 12 months are subject to tax for individual taxpayers.

Also all the expenses of holding and improving assets will attract some form of tax benefit, through outright deduction, progressive write off or offset against future capital profits.

Australia also has a very attractive taxation system in place for retirement incomes, with the announcement in the 2006 Federal Budget that Pensions and Lump Sums from Australian Superannuation funds will be tax free from 1st July 2007.

We also possess a tax advantaged company dividend system, referred to as Imputation, which can provide the means to cover any potential tax expense.

In short, there are many options available to you under the Australian system which may seem somewhat complicated, but are there to ensure a fair burden of taxation in the community.

The key is, making the decisions rather than dealing with the consequences.

Your time as an Expat, gives you the opportunity to control your Australian tax future.

With sensible and legal planning, a tax-free life in Australia is indeed possible.

Swimming with the tide can indeed be rewarding.

6. To Be Or Not To Be...A Resident

Once you have decided to take an overseas posting, the first question is normally one of whether you remain a tax resident or become a non-resident for Australian tax purposes.

Many people incorrectly assume that they have a choice as to which one to maintain.

This is not the case. Residency is a matter of law and fact.

It is particularly important to know whether or not you are non-resident.

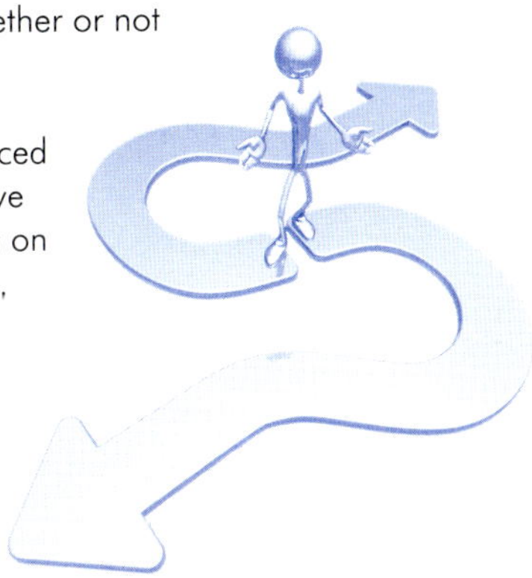

As a non-resident, only Australian sourced income will be taxable and you will have the ability to accrue valuable tax losses on negatively geared property investments.

On the other hand, as a resident all your worldwide income and capital gains remains subject to tax. This may include your overseas salary if you do not remain abroad for more than 90 days at a time.

In truth, the question of residency is one we can all answer ourselves.

In deciding which you may be, the test revolves around where you "live" in the true sense of the word.

In the past the number of days spent in a particular place was a key issue, in modern times this is not the case.

The key criterion is where is your "life" located, such as your career, your permanent dwelling, your family and your primary personal belongings.

The tax office has issued rulings on this topic with examples for circumstances where people are not taking up a permanent long-term position, and there may be some grey areas in determining which status applies and the tax consequences that may be relevant.

However, it is safe to say that anyone taking up a long-term position, say more than twelve months, and relocating their family and "life" to an overseas destination shall be deemed a Non-Resident for tax purposes.

It should also be noted that a husband and wife can have different status in regards to residency if they are in fact living apart for work purposes or children's education.

We all know where we live, just don't be afraid to admit it to the Australian Tax Office.

Everyone's circumstances are different so do not be afraid to seek specialised advice if you are not sure as to which will apply to you.

In short, honestly ask yourself where is your current HOME today, and normally that is where you are resident for tax purposes.

7. Understanding Your Privilege

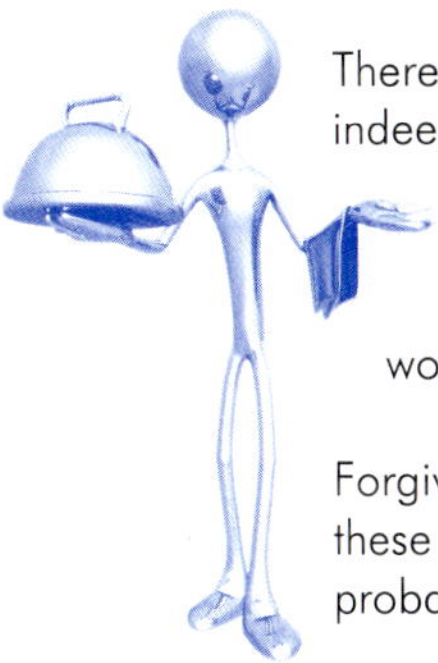

There are many reasons why the Australian Expatriate is indeed "The Luckiest Person on Earth".

Sometimes we need a simple reminder of how lucky we are as it is easily forgotten in the hectic life of working abroad.

Forgive my simplicity in bringing these to your attention, when you probably already know them too

Privilege is often only evident once it is lost.

Automatic Re Entry

As an Australian citizen you can return whenever you want.

Just about everyone in the world is pressing hard to get in and migration to Australia is going to be one of the top "things I must do" for many people on this planet.

Regardless of where you came from in Australia, we would all agree that there are few places as affordable, environmentally clean and as socially safe as Australia.

I have travelled far and wide and still yet to find a place that has the overall appeal of Australia. We just need a better taxation system and more robust economy and it would be paradise.

I cannot do much to change the economy but I can change the way you look at the tax system.

Global Experiences

By leaving Australia you have gone in search of experience that was somewhat lacking in Australia.

Every day you are now interacting with people that have a very different outlook to our friends and colleagues that we have left in Australia.

This will have a more profound effect on your views than you may think.

Embrace these experiences for as long as you can. Remember you are not in Australia now, you are the visitor, so take full advantage of this learning period of your life and understand that we are part of a real global revolution where one day we will all just be "earthlings".

Opportunity of a Lifetime

By having the courage to leave the comfort of your home country, you are rewarded with opportunity, both personally and financially.

What you may not have truly realised is that these opportunities can and will follow you back to Australia when you eventually return.

Global business is on a far greater scale than in Australia so the knowledge gained will be invaluable to Australian employers when you return, albeit that they might not be able to afford to match your Expat salary package.

Friendships that you make in your time abroad may well last and grow into business opportunities on your return to Australia.

Many of our clients have established successful Australian-based operations for friends or business contacts made during their time as an expatriate.

The possibility of new trade of goods or services when you relocate to Australia, are endless if you keep your ears open to the sound of opportunity.

Earning Power

It is true to say that most expatriates would be earning more abroad than they did in Australia.

This is further enhanced by the fact that many are also in lower personal taxation regimes than at home.

This additional earning power is the key to your financial future if you use it wisely.

I have always told my clients that "the experience alone is not enough" for the time that you are an expatriate.

If you are not gaining in a financial sense then you need to reassess where you are heading and try and find someway of keeping some of the extra earning power you have.

If you can, all these privileges will indeed ensure you remain "The Luckiest Person on Earth".

8. Gaining Control

Gaining control of our lives is a very difficult task for us all.

As an expatriate your workload no doubt keeps you very busy, then throw in the family, travel commitments, social requirements and trying to keep in touch with everyone back home, it is indeed difficult to find the time or inclination to actually sit down and give some thought to controlling your financial present and future.

No one else can make you change your behaviour. It is your choice and your personal benefit.

The good news for you is that it is actually a very simple task and one that you can effortlessly bring into your day-to-day life without disrupting your normal routine.

There are a few simple tips that you need to understand and follow, that will allow you to gain control of your financial life as an expatriate.

Advance Knowledge

Arming yourself with knowledge is critical in the financial survival stakes.

Fortunately for you, simply reading this book is probably going to give you enough knowledge to work your way through the maze when it comes to your Australian taxation issues.

You also need to know as much as you deem appropriate about a number of things including;

- Safe investing
- Tax status in country of earning
- Job security and opportunities
- Australian career markets for return
- Personal goals and objectives

The support structure available to expatriates is ever expanding so in most cases you will be able to find well-qualified and reputable advisors to assist.

As with most things in life, there is no substitute for experience, so simply talking amongst your fellow expatriates can provide you with enough guideposts to make it through.

The Internet is a very important tool that can also unlock some hard to answer questions so invest some time "surfing".

Known Time Lines, In Sections

Another good fortune for most expatriates is the fact that when we do our planning, we generally have clear time lines in which to work with.

This is mainly true as most expatriates are on set contracts, albeit that they are very often extended.

Knowing that you have a certain amount of years as an expatriate, is important in deciding how aggressive you may need to be in your savings or investment strategy.

Obviously the more time abroad the better as you can spread your plan over many years, rather than cram it into a few years.

Children will also have a major impact on your planning. Many expatriates choose to return to Australia when their children reach school age, so this once more allows you to quickly and easily identify the remaining planning period.

Be honest and frank with your partner and yourself in identifying these time lines as they become increasingly important. Particularly if you have already let a few good years slip by.

Saving Power

This is the single most important aspect of gaining control of your financial future.

Saving Power is often greatly over estimated by expatriates as it is commonly confused with disposable income.

For the record, disposable income is your salary or earnings less taxation.

Saving Power is simply defined as your disposable income (salary after tax) less lifestyle spending.

Regardless of how much you earn after tax, it is worthless if you spend every cent!

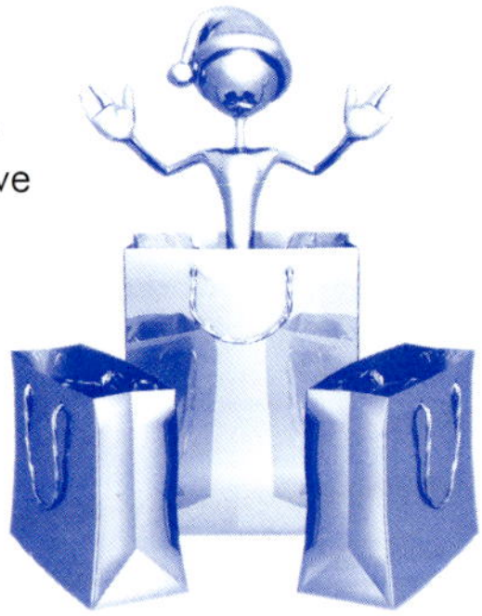

Lifestyle spending is usually where we all get into trouble, after all we deserve to spend on ourselves.

I will be honest in telling you that in 20 years of accounting, I have yet to win an argument where lifestyle was pitted against financial considerations. Lifestyle always wins.

In reality this is not really a problem unless it gets out of control.

As I mentioned earlier in the book, it is very common in the first few years as an expatriate to reward yourself, and far be it from me to overly discourage you.

Just be aware of the long-term impact and make sure you really want it.

I have a great job, I get to make people happy though sensible tax planning.

What you earn is essentially irrelevant. It's what you keep that really matters.

The only time I am sad at work is when a long time expatriate comes to see me for the first time and is heading back to Australia tomorrow. In many cases, these people can have an abundance of trinkets and toys, a lifetime of pleasant holiday memories and an awesome wardrobe.

Unfortunately they never took control of their spending so they have saved a tidy sum that is a fraction of what it could have been. The opportunity to save is now drastically reduced as they return to the Australian income tax system unprepared.

You will see as we progress, the advantages they have missed out on. Let's hope you do not follow suit.

Another of my favourite sayings is that the holiday won't pay for the house, but the house will pay for the holiday.

Next time you consider an excessive lifestyle spending, consider how much sweeter that item would be if it was coming from the profit on your investments or rental from your property!

If you can monitor and manage your lifestyle spending and redirect excesses towards investment, the speed that you build wealth will dramatically increase.

Enjoy yourself today, but don't forget tomorrow.

Commit Yourself

At some point in time you must make a serious commitment to your family and yourself to gain control for your own personal benefit.

This is indeed hard, but no harder than the commitment you have already made in leaving your beloved country, family and friends, and braving the world.

You can do it. Spend a little less, save a little more. I suppose it is like starting a "financial diet". If you're generally good, chocolate every now and then won't tip the scales so just be sensible and you will be fine.

Setting realistic targets and monitoring the results will keep you encouraged.

Tax Effectiveness

Saving is a hard task at the best of times. Any advantage you can achieve to help boost your wealth should be pursued as long as it is a safe and sensible option.

It is important to understand the difference between something that is tax effective and a tax scheme.

Tax effective simply means an investment with acknowledged taxation incentives known and easily applied.

A tax scheme is an arrangement that questions the law in its application in order to seek advantage through a favourable interpretation that is usually untested against the tax authority.

Many people forget that under Australian taxation law, the tax department has enormous power that allows it to look through any scheme and tax as if it was not there. As mentioned in chapter 5, do not swim against the tide.

Prudent investment can only be improved with a sensible tax effective strategy, as you will see in later chapters.

Addressing these issues will give you the best chance of gaining control of your financial life and making a life changing impact on your future.

9. Leaving Australia

In developing any long-term strategy, we must start with a strong foundation.

As such we shall first deal with the taxation issues that need to be dealt with when you first leave Australia.

The Australian taxation system requires all Resident Taxpayers to lodge an Income Tax Return each year, including one in the year of departure from Australia, and some specific issues need to be addressed.

Should your overseas work be limited to short term contracts or transitory fly in, fly out arrangements, you should seek additional advice, as the matters discussed may not apply to you. Refer to Chapter 6 dealing with the question of residency.

If you do consider yourself living overseas, read on, as the information you are about to gain will prove invaluable in the years ahead.

Make sure you consider your exist issues at the time you leave.

Once you have acknowledged that you are indeed becoming a Non-Resident for Australian taxation purposes, these matters need to be considered.

Part Year Income

Your Income Tax Return in the year of departure will need to include all normal income such as salaries, interest, dividends, Australian rental with the usual offset for any allowable deductions you would normally claim against this income, covering the period up to the date of departure.

Your return will in essence be very similar to a normal tax year, however you will only be entitled to the annual tax free threshold (currently A$6,000) on a pro rata basis for the period you were actually resident.

Importantly, your income from salary or investment earned outside of Australia will not need to be declared in this or any subsequent Income Tax Return whilst you remain overseas and Non-Resident of Australia for tax purposes.

Should you be receiving income from Australian sources through business, consulting fees or rental, this will need to be declared regardless of whether you received before or after your departure.

Withholding Tax

As a non-resident, interest and dividends received after your departure date do not need to be included in your income tax return. You must notify the bank or company and inform them that you are now a non-resident.

Any interest or dividends received once you are living out of Australia become subject to a Withholding Tax only and are no longer subject to Income Tax.

You should note that it is illegal to not have Withholding Tax deducted so make sure you take the time to let the paying institution know.

The banks should automatically deduct 10% from your interest when it is credited to your account.

Companies paying you a dividend are not required to deduct any Withholding Tax if the company is declaring a "Fully Franked Dividend". That is basically a dividend paid from after tax earnings of the company.

Where the dividend is paid from untaxed profits, a Withholding Tax of 15% or 30% will apply. The lower rate applies in countries that have reciprocal tax arrangements with Australia, which are most Western countries.

Should you be required to declare the interest or dividends in your new country, you will normally be credited for any withholding tax paid in Australia.

Capital Gains Tax

The current law provides for some assets held by individuals leaving Australia and becoming Non-Residents to be deemed as sold on the date of departure.

Real Estate assets are not affected by this rule and remain subject to Capital Gains Tax when eventually sold.

The deemed sale of non-real estate assets, such as shares, can create a tax liability that may not be welcomed.

You should note that if you have held the asset for longer than 12 months, then only half of any deemed sale capital gain would be taxable.

This can be waived by an election in your Income Tax Return deferring the Capital Gains Tax until a future taxable event, such as the actual sale, at some later point. It is important to note that if NO election is made the assets are deemed sold.

The decision to have the deemed sale or deferment should be made with thorough analysis with your professional adviser to decide which is the best in the circumstances.

It is important to note that once you become a non-resident, most investment assets (except property) become free of Capital Gains Tax whilst overseas, if tax has been paid up to the date of change in residence.

There is no quick easy answer to which option is best as all our circumstances are very different. The importance of you making the right choice is critical, so make sure you give the matter due consideration and do not get forced into an unfavourable position.

Superannuation

When you leave Australia, you will have to make some decisions in regard to any Superannuation benefits you have built up. This may include rolling over existing benefits or to cash in policies.

In some limited cases you may be able to withdraw some or all of your built-up entitlements. This may include permanent departure from Australia or financial hardship.

In most cases it is best to leave your superannuation intact for your eventual return.

There is no major advantage in making contributions whilst you are abroad as no tax deduction is likely to be available, but that does not mean it should not be considered.

Advice should be sought from your Superannuation consultant as the laws in this regard are somewhat complicated and vary depending on the style of superannuation fund you currently hold.

Family Home

A decision is usually made on whether to rent the family home whilst abroad.

Leaving the house vacant during your absence is an expensive luxury that should be carefully assessed. The lost rent should be weighed up against the actual usage of the house if you would prefer to keep it as a holiday home.

The annual rent will pay for alternative accommodation at a lovely hotel during your holiday period and may be even fund another property purchase.

The additional rental income is usually welcomed however it will be a taxable income and must be reported each year. Importantly all costs in relation to owning a property are claimable and offset any tax.

This includes interest on your existing mortgage, which in many cases can ensure that any tax liability on the rental income will be minimised.

If you have recently built the home or carried out any major renovations in the years prior to your relocation, there may well be substantial depreciation allowances available to you now that the property is rented.

In most cases the Capital Gains Tax free status of the Principal Residence can carry on even during a temporary absence of up to six years, regardless of whether or not you move back in.

Your family home can remain free of Capital Gains Tax for 6 years even if it is rented out.

Beyond the six years the property may become subject to Capital Gains Tax if you have not returned to Australia. This will be on a pro rata basis.

For example if you had lived in the house for three years prior to leaving, rented it out for eight years and then sold it without returning to Australia, you would be entitled to the Capital Gains exemption pro rata on nine years (three years occupation plus six year entitlement) over the total ownership period of 11 years.

This can be a major benefit reducing any potential Capital Gains Tax.

If the property was first rented out after 20th August 1996, then you may also be able to use the Market Value on the date of first rental as your cost base for tax purposes, and then have the 6-year exemption apply from that point on.

This may be of some benefit if you have been overseas for a substantial period of time after the 6-year tax-free period, and believe that the gains prior to rental were more significant than those since you left Australia and stopped using the property as your residence.

It is important to note that you must have actually lived in the house prior to moving outside in order to qualify for the 6-year exemption. In the same way, a trip home to buy the property would not qualify you.

When you return to Australia, the 6 years will cease when you replace the property with another residence, or move back into it and therefore have it qualify as your Principal Place of Residence once again.

Also, you can only ever have one residence per family.

If you do eventually sell your family home at a future time, deciding the correct tax treatment can be a somewhat complicated decision, and one that should be undertaken with professional advice.

However, the concessions in the system are there to ensure you do pay the least amount of tax possible.

Higher Education Contribution Scheme (HECS)

Any HECS debt at the time of departure will continue to be due.

Your HECS debt is usually repaid when your taxable income exceeds certain amounts, starting at $36,800 at the time of writing.

If you do not have any Taxable Australian income while you live abroad, then there will be no requirement to repay the loan unless you wish to make a voluntary payment.

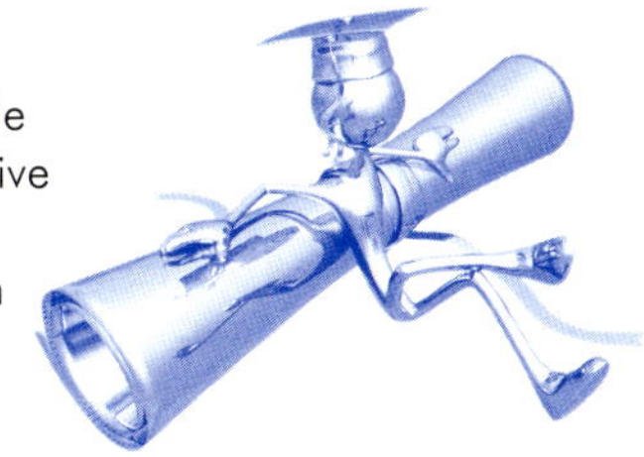

Recent changes to the repayment rules, mean that if you have an Australian rental property, the loss may be treated as an income for HECS calculation purposes so this may have a bearing on your repayment of this loan sooner than expected.

Having dealt with these matters you can now look forward to maximising planning benefits available to you whilst working abroad, with a clear conscious and new found understanding.

10. Whilst You're Away

Whatever reason you became an expatriate does not matter. What does is making the most of the time you are abroad.

The key points to remember are:

- **Save Sensibly**, make sure you are keeping some of your hard earned salary for tomorrow.
- **Set Real Targets**, ones that you can achieve and monitor your progress. Identify the things you want whilst both abroad and on your return.
- **Control Lifestyle Spending**, at least as best you can.
- **Be Wary of Tax Schemes**, they generally only offer risk and no reward. There are always better options.

Your salary income will be taxed in the country you are living in and each place will have its own rules. Make sure you get good "local" advice to protect you from any tax issues you may face on that front.

From an Australian perspective, you are basically now only taxed on Australian sourced income. This for most of us will just be property.

Changing your future on return to Australia, is shaped by the choices you make while an Expat

If you are living in a low tax regime and have managed to "gain control" of your finances, then you have probably moved from the spend to save phase and are starting to wonder what to do with your newfound wealth.

Some of the places savings are directed to are reviewed as follows:

Debt Reduction

After living in a high debt world in Australia, struggling with the home mortgage and credit cards, it is common for many expatriates to aggressively reduce debt as their first priority.

Clearing any private non-property debt should be first in line. This would include credit cards and personal loans.

These loans have no tax benefits and often have high interest rates, so clearing them is always a good idea before you attempt to reduce any other loans.

Reducing debt on the family home or other investment property is another option but not always a recommended one.

This is because loans on income producing property hold substantial tax benefits and these should be maintained and any reduction should be made when you return to Australia.

We look at this in more detail later in Chapter 12.

However should you have a loan on a property that you do not foresee renting out at some future date, such as a personal residence or a holiday house, then these loans should also be targeted for reduction.

Some people also have loans on shares, and these may become non-tax deductible if you have had the Deemed Disposal as the income and growth is now non taxable, so no deduction can be claimed.

If you insist on reducing debt, make sure you get it in the right order of repayment being;

> *Firstly, to any private loans and credit cards,*
> *Then any share or investment trust loans,*
> *Then to any non- income producing property loans,*
> *Next to any loan on a property that you may potentially live in, and*
> *Finally, against any loan on an income producing property only once you are sure that you have no other better use for the money.*

By following these repayment rules in sequence, you will ensure that non tax-deductible loans are kept to a minimum, whilst you maximise your tax effective borrowings.

Cash Deposits

Always a favourite. Funds held in Australia will have a Withholding Tax of 10% deducted from the interest.

If you hold the deposits overseas, then any interest earned while you live out of Australia will have no tax implication in Australia, but may be taxable in the country you are living in.

You could also consider using an "Offset Account" if you have some loans with an Australian Bank, as this is a very effective way of reducing your interest cost, whilst at the same time keeping access to your money.

This can be particularly useful in saving for your eventual residence when you return to Australia, and is a viable option to fixed deposits or cash savings accounts.

There are no tax implications in Australia of transferring money in or out of the country.

Australian Property

The taxation benefits of Australian property investment are detailed in Chapter 11 "The Power of Property".

Australian property still offers some of the best value for money of any investment choice in the world, and given it is what most expatriates know best and feel most comfortable with, it is not surprising to find it at the top of most investment lists.

It will always remain a favourite investment option for expatriates, and rightly so.

Australian Shares

Acquiring Australian shares whilst overseas is also a very effective saving strategy for most expatriates.

This is especially true when you consider that property loans should be paid off very gradually, if at all, and therefore cash built up must be invested somewhere.

Selection is always the hardest part but assuming you seek appropriate advice, the tax benefits again make this a good savings option.

For non-residents, virtually all public company shares trading whilst overseas is free of tax and therefore no Capital Gains Tax will apply.

This does not extend to private companies, which remain taxable.

Dividends that the company has paid Company Tax on (normally referred to as "Fully Franked") will be given free of tax, whilst if no tax has been paid by the company, a withholding tax of 15% will be levied.

When you return to Australia, the shares will become subject to tax, but only on gains made in excess of the Market Value on the date of returning to Australia as a resident.

This can work well, as it is usually a good option to sell the shares on return in order to realise funds to clear a mortgage or purchase the property we intend to live in.

If this is done at or soon after arrival, this can ensure that no Capital Gains tax is payable on the profits made on the shareholding whilst overseas.

Shares can also be a very effective source of retirement income, so if you do not need to sell the shares, they will be a welcomed tax effective investment when you return.

Australian Private Companies or Trusts

There is often the opportunity to establish an Australian Private Company or Family Trust to hold your newfound savings.

In fact some people also wonder whether to acquire property in these structures.

Use of these structures is usually not recommended until you return to Australia as they may in fact make an otherwise non taxable investment, fully taxable, as the company or trust may be deemed resident and taxed on worldwide income.

In addition the 50% Capital Gains tax exemption does not apply to companies, so generally it is not recommended to hold assets that may appreciate in value through a company.

This area should always be discussed and undertaken with professional advice.

Non Australian Shares & Trusts

The same rules apply to Non Australian shares as for Australian, that is no Australian Tax will apply to Non-Residents.

Again, tax will begin to accrue only on the gains from the increase in market value on the date of return.

Some special rules do apply to a select group of investments in non-public trusts, where the capital gains may be taxable each year on an accrual basis.

This area is very complicated and you should seek expert advice on a case-by-case basis to be sure of the potential tax implications.

Many of the financial plans being offered to Australian expatriates are designed for non-Australians. As such they may well be effective while you remain offshore but could be a major problem when you return.

Ensure you ask how the Australian tax authorities look at the plan for people living in Australia unless you do not intend to still have the fund when you return.

Superannuation and Pension Savings Plans

There have been many changes in the Australian Superannuation system since the 2006 Federal Budget.

Effectively from 1st July 2007, all pensions and lump sums from Australian Taxed Superannuation Funds will be tax free to recipients in Australia.

This is something to look forward to you on your return, and combined with the other benefits discussed in this book, should mean that you will never need to pay tax in Australia during your retirement.

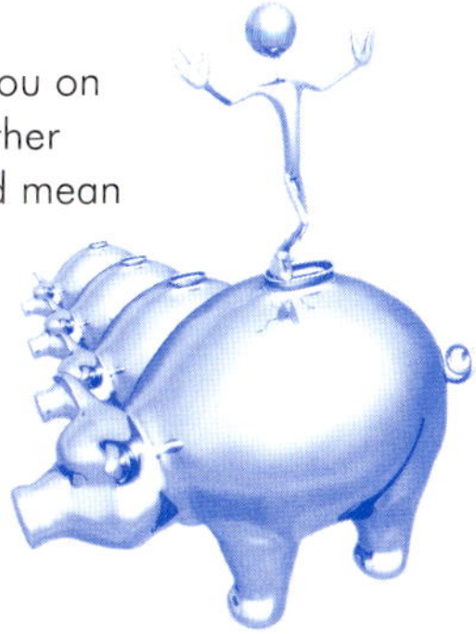

Putting money into Super whilst you are overseas may be a viable and sensible option depending on your age and circumstances.

If your overseas employer makes contributions to a Pension Fund on your behalf, then it may be best to see if they can indeed contribute to an Australian Fund for your future benefit.

The issues surrounding Superannuation are very complicated and beyond the scope of this book.

It may not be advantageous to contribute to a fund whilst overseas, as the deductions may not be able to be claimed as a tax deduction, and it may create investments (such as shares) to be held in a taxable environment rather than tax-free in your personal name.

If you do decide to contribute, it is important to advise the fund whether you have in fact claimed a tax deduction or not, as getting this wrong may mean that you are charged the 15% Contributions Tax unnecessarily.

At the time of writing this edition, the rules are in constant change as the new announcements are worked through parliament, so keep an eye on things before making permanent decisions.

Needless to say that it is something that should be discussed with a qualified advisor and an appropriate strategy established.

Other Non Australian Assets

Any other assets acquired whilst overseas such as non-Australian property or antiques, will also become taxable in Australia once you return as a tax resident.

Again any future capital gains tax will only be levied on the increase in the market value on the date of return.

With this knowledge it is essential to obtain a sworn valuation on these assets at the time of return to avoid any problems in the future to establish the market price.

As you may well have noticed, that almost everything besides Australian property is tax free in Australia whilst you live abroad. I must say that you cannot get any more tax effective than nil, or can you?

This should not be your primary consideration though, as all will have tax implications upon your eventual return to Australia.

The built up value of your savings may be tax free, but the future income and capital gains received will have to be declared once you become an Australian resident taxpayer once again.

You also need to address the important issue of what the tax consequences are in the country that you are working in, as each location will have different rules.

Too many people lose sight that as investor your main objective is to have a good investment, not eliminate your tax.

It is generally accepted that a spread of investment types is usually best.

As an expatriate you will be spoilt for choice when it comes to investment options, so work your way through the confusion and hopefully you will be successful.

My favourite has always been Australian property...

11. The Power Of Property

It is not my role to convince you to acquire Australian property from an investment perspective.

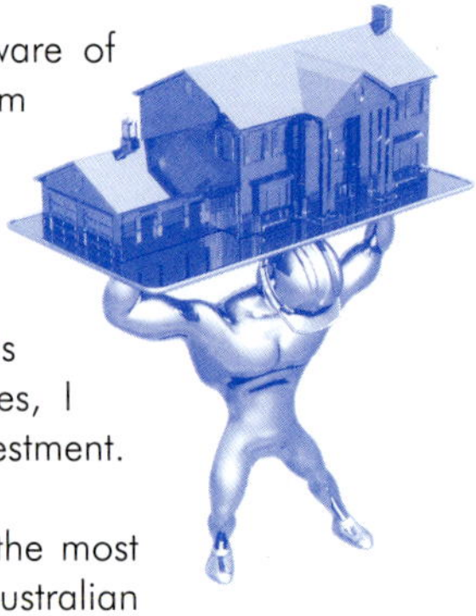

As an expatriate you are no doubt very aware of property markets in Australia, particularly from your home city, and probably could tell me what is best.

As a property investor myself and with the good fortune I have had in advising thousands of property investors on their taxation issues, I know too well the value of property as an investment.

Property is the most tangible and arguably the most successful form of investing in the world. Australian property has also demonstrated itself as one of the most consistent markets in the world.

As I write this book, the recent figures released by the Real Estate Institute of Australia, show that every major Australian Capital City had grown by in excess of 9% p.a. over the 10 years to June 2006.

I will expand on some tips I have learned from listening and watching my successful clients in Chapter 15 – Leave out the Lemons.

Property ownership offers many tax advantages: just as well we love doing it.

Not only is Australian investment property a popular investment choice for many expatriates, it is also the best tax planning tool whilst overseas and is a wise way to have forced savings.

This is because it is usually your only taxable activity whilst you are overseas.

Negative Gearing – Expat Style

If you are familiar with the term "negative gearing" then you will understand the tax benefits that were available to you whilst working in Australia.

Put as simply as possible, negative gearing is the deliberate use of borrowed funds to acquire an asset where the income is not enough to cover the holding costs and interest creating an annual deficit, or negative. This is done solely on the expectation of capital appreciation of the asset being greater than this negative so that overall real wealth is created.

If you were still living and working in Australia, this negative gearing would legally help reduce the income tax on your salary or other income, and is still regarded as one of the most cost effective tax planning methods.

This is especially true since the Howard Government announced that only half of any capital gains would be subject to taxation, if assets were held longer than twelve months.

As an expatriate, this annual deficit has nothing to offset so simply accumulates each year you are away to be used at some future time.

I call the accumulated amount "tax credits", and the great thing about them is that they go on indefinitely until such time as you need them to offset either future rental surplus, capital gains on sale or to offset Australian taxable income when you return to Australia.

This may include salary or retirement incomes.

These tax credits should not be underestimated in their future value to the expatriate, especially when you consider that the top marginal tax rate in Australia is 46.5% (including Medicare).

When in Australia, you can negative gear into any type of asset, including shares, however as you are living abroad other activities are not taxable in Australia you will not be able to claim your interest costs in Australia while you are overseas and therefore cannot accumulate tax credits.

Only property will allow this benefit during your time overseas.

That is not to say that borrowing to invest in shares and other investments should not be done, it just means that you will receive no tax advantages so it is essential the asset performs better than the interest cost.

In Who's Name?

As a rule, your property should always be acquired in an individual's name.

This ensures the 50% Capital Gains Tax exemption once the property is owned more than 12 months and also ensures the Tax Credits built up remain in your personal name.

Using a Trust or Company may quarantine the losses in the structure and not allow them to offset your salary when you eventually return to Australia.

There may be some particular reasons to use Trusts or Companies such as Legal Protection or Estate Planning, and these need to be considered with specialised advice to ensure that using any entity will in fact be in your best interests rather than just complicating your affairs unnecessarily.

It can be beneficial to use entities for commercial purchases in some cases, and again advice should be sought.

It is not very often that using an entity would be a better option than your personal name, so be careful not to be using entities just out of fear or because you heard a rumour that they may be better.

As a couple, it is usually the simplest to acquire in joint names if this is how you prefer to own the assets.

This will ensure that you can spread any potential tax against two marginal tax rates ensuring the maximum low tax rates available.

There are some cases when it may be better to acquire the property in one person's name such as if your partner does not expect to have any salary earnings upon return to Australia or due to family or other issues.

By having the property in the expected income earners name, any tax credits built up will be in that name and be able to offset that person's salary income on return to Australia.

This may be particularly important from a cash flow perspective in order to maximise your tax deductions and minimise your after-tax holding costs.

This needs to be weighed against the potential benefit of a lower income tax rate which may be better to hold the property in joint names if the debt on the property is quite low and if you envisage selling the property for a large gain in the near future.

Debt Management

Only Australian property offers you the option to build tax credits whilst abroad. It is one of the reasons we recommend paying cash for non-property investments (shares, unit trusts, etc) and borrowing to acquire Australian property.

It is important that you should borrow at reasonably high levels, say 60-80% finance, to maximise the tax advantages available.

I will prove the merit of financing in Chapter 12, but for now you should just take my word for it that it makes good financial sense when it comes to acquiring Australian property.

In reality, most of us have to borrow, as to pay cash is a luxury we cannot afford, at least not yet.

Buying Power

This time of your life is no doubt when your buying power is at it's greatest.

Not only are you on an expatriate salary and most likely low income tax, but you are also a landlord.

When you combine your earnings with the rent, you will be amazed at what level of property you can afford.

Premium suburbs, beachfront houses, penthouses all become affordable to you now.

When you were in Australia these types of property may well have been just dreams, but they are now within your grasp.

Take advantage of this time to build a high quality portfolio, before you return to Australia.

You may well find that your only limitation will be deposit, which will encourage you to save diligently or exploit the equity you may already have in an existing property.

Is Your Loan Tax Deductible?

One of the most important issues in maximising your taxation benefits is confirming that the property loan interest is in fact tax deductible.

The key here is where the original loan proceeds went, not where the security is held.

For example, if your original loan was drawn at the acquisition of the property and paid to the vendor, then tax-deductible status will remain on the loan throughout.

However if you had at some later date drawn some of your excess repayments on your home loan and used them for a holiday or other private purpose, then that portion of your loan (on a pro rata basis) would not be allowed as a tax deduction.

This is an important fact to realise, as the only way to ensure deduction is for the loan proceeds to be used to acquire, or improve, an income producing property, either the current property, or a subsequent purchase.

This is true regardless of whether you borrow from any source either in or out of Australia.

If you have a property that has had its loan substantially reduced over the years, you may find that there is an excess of security available that can be used to assist in the purchase of your next investment property.

This refinancing option can be used to great effect in your tax planning strategies and can preserve your cash holdings for other uses, whilst at the same time enabling you to build a substantial portfolio of income producing, tax effective property.

I remind you of earlier sections where we discussed the deductibility of loans for shares and other investments.

Ensuring that your cash is directed to shares and other non-taxable investments, and appropriate borrowings are taken out to acquire your Australian income producing property investments, then you will be able to ensure that you achieve the maximum tax benefits whilst abroad.

Swimming with the Tide

In an earlier chapter I spoke of working with the system.

There are times when the tide can flow stronger in certain places than others, as the government offers special incentives to encourage you to take a certain path.

These incentives are there to ensure that funds are directed to areas that have maximum benefit to the economy as a whole and it makes sense for the government to tempt you in certain directions.

Once you have decided to invest in Australian property, there are some additional encouragements for you.

New & Near New Property

The general tax benefits available are further enhanced by some additional incentives afforded to new and near new property with an allowance for depreciation on fittings and a special allowance to deduct the construction costs.

On new buildings and those built for rental after 1985, the write off is an attractive 2.5% of the original construction cost, available each year for 40 years.

In most cases this can enhance the build up of tax losses (tax credits) by as much as 35% without incurring any additional cash outlay.

Buildings that commenced constructed between August 1984 and September 1987 were entitled to a 4% depreciation rate (25 years) as a special incentive at that time.

In the same way, Short Term Stay accommodation may also qualify for the 4% depreciation, however this style of property usually offers a higher risk on resale, hence the encouragement offered by the government.

These building depreciation amounts pass between each owner of the property, so you should always check with your vendor just in case.

Furthermore depreciation allowances on the fittings in the property can also boost the build up of losses substantially. This will obviously depend on the value of the fit out and age of the property.

For apartments an additional depreciation write off is available for the common fittings in the property such as the swimming pool, foyers and elevators.

It goes without saying that the newer the building the greater the tax benefits available.

The motivation here is to ensure that your purchase creates jobs and economic activity, and also the government happily collects the additional GST Revenue on new property acquisition.

Coincidently, foreign buyers are only allowed by law to acquire new property, so they by default gain the maximum deductions.

Off the Plan

In the much the same way, "Off the Plan" acquisitions provide an additional incentive for the astute investor and tax planner.

Not only do they offer the highest level of tax write offs (because they are brand new) but they allow a level of forward planning to be introduced as it pre programs future acquisitions into the tax plan being implemented.

By making the forward commitment a level of discipline is introduced to ensure a savings program is adhered to.

It may also be possible to save some money in Stamp Duty when you buy house and land separately, as the duty may be levled only on the land component in many circumstances.

In addition, Victoria offers another incentive in so far as the Stamp Duty levied on property purchases is significantly reduced for Off the Plan purchases.

This is because the duty is levied on the progressive value of the project rather than the total sale price on completion as in other states.

This saving can amount to many thousands of dollars and is indeed worthy of consideration.

Travel for Inspection

As you are living overseas, when you legitimately travel back to Australia to inspect your investment property you may claim the expenses incurred.

These include airfares, accommodation, meals and car hire.

To claim your airfare in full, the purpose of the trip must have been predominantly relating to the property, for example, Off changing tenants or undertaking renovations.

Where the trip has a dual purpose, property and holiday, then the airfare can be claimed on a pro rata basis.

Importantly, you must keep a diary of your activities to substantiate your claim.

Wherever prudent, the additional allowances of building write off and depreciation should be sought, but not at the expense of quality and value.

The long-term taxation benefits associated with Australian property should not be underestimated.

When you combine the fact that you can acquire quality Australian property at current day prices, not the increased value when you return, while at the same time building a large protection against future income and capital gains tax it is clear as to why Australian property is an extremely important investment and should be integral in every expatriates financial planning whilst overseas.

Before you get excited and rush out to buy loads of Australian property, I must remind you of two important issues.

Future Debt Reduction

At some time in the future you are going to have to repay the loans you take out. This can only be done through savings or sale of assets.

A lot will depend on whether you see the property as a short or long-term asset.

If the property is bought with an expectation to sell in a few years at a profit, then it will look after its own debt reduction from the sale proceeds.

Alternatively, if you intend on using the rent to fund your retirement, then you need to be putting away savings to pay out the remainder of the loan. Importantly, I would not significantly reduce the loan until such time as you need the rental income.

Servicing

Negative Gearing is a great concept and it does work.

The key to its success is in making sure you can afford the annual holding cost, so you can reap the reward of the future capital profits.

As a general rule we recommend that you use no more than 40% of your real savings power to fund the servicing of negative gearing.

Real Savings is simply defined as the actual savings you are achieving, rather than what you hope to save. How much have you in the bank and invested today less what was there a year ago, and then add back what your existing Australian property cost you as well.

By allocating only 40% of this amount you will ensure that you are still building up cash or liquid savings that will protect you against unforseen events such as rental vacancy, job shifting, renovations, major repairs and life's normal challenges.

It will also allow funds to build up for the important task of paying out or acquiring your future Australian residence when you return to Australia.

Being too aggressive may compromise your lifestyle and ability to save for your eventual residence.

You should also be clear as to your intentions, mainly because affording all the loans may be much harder when you return to Australia at some future time.

PURCHASE ANALYSIS

VALUE OF LAND	$ 180,000				
VALUE OF BUILDING	$ 220,000				
TOTAL PACKAGE	$ 400,000	Finance	80%	AMOUNT	$320,000
		Term (yrs)	30		
BORROWING COSTS	$ 2,280	Rate	7.37%	Monthly Repayment	($2,209)
SETTLEMENT & STAMP DUTY	$ 16,000				
				CLIENT CONTRIBUTION	
TOTAL INVESTMENT	$ 418,280	Less FINANCE	$320,000		$98,280

ANNUAL CASH FLOW & TAXATION SUMMARY

INCOME						
Rent Received	per week	$385			$ 20,000	
OWNERSHIP EXPENSES						
Taxation Return Fee				350		
Agent Management Fee			8.25%	1,650		
Council, Water & Land Tax				2,000		
Maintenance or Body Corporate				2,500		
Insurance				165		
Interest	Rate	7.37%		23,584		
					$ 30,249	
NET CASH POSITION BEFORE PRINCIPAL REPAYMENT					($10,249)	($ 854) Monthly Cash Contribution ($ 244) Principal Repayment ($1,098) Total Monthly Contribution
OVERSEAS EXPENSES (OPTIONAL OUTLAY)						
Travel for Inspection				2,000		
Telephone, Fax & Stationary				300		
					$ 2,300	
TAX INCENTIVES (NON CASH OUTLAY)						
Building Write Off						
- Building Cost @		2.50%		5,500		
Depreciation						
- Average 15%p.a. on		$25,000		3,750		
Borrowing Expenses written off				456		
					$ 9,706	
TAXABLE INCOME / (LOSS)					($22,255)	

KEY INVESTMENT STATISTICS

MINIMUM ANNUAL PROPERTY GROWTH REQUIRED:

1. TO COVER CASH SHORTFALL	2.56%	P.A.
2. WITH NO CAPITAL GAINS TAX	11.13%	P.A.

Now is a good time to look at a typical example.

We have developed our own customised software, The Property Tax Estimator, which applies for overseas-based investors.

In this case, we are going to acquire a brand new A$400,000 apartment, which is providing 5% p.a. gross rental.

Do not be too concerned if this figure is below or above your spending range as the proportions are the important issue, and they remain fairly consistent throughout Australia.

You are welcome to visit our websites at either ***www.smats.net*** or ***www.aussieproperty.com*** where you can create your own customised Estimator prepared for the property you own or are looking to purchase. This is free of charge and done instantly.

We are going to finance this property to 80% of its value and put in the required 20% equity and pay all purchase costs from our savings.

As an expatriate you can borrow up to 100% of the purchase price of property through a select amount of lenders.

In doing this, the loan may be more expensive as you will be required to pay Mortgage Insurance and possible higher establishment fees and interest rates.

I would only do this if it were absolutely necessary in order to secure a quality property, as the additional borrowing increases the risk.

For the sake of a general example we are going to consider the 80% lending ratio and as such you can see that you need A$98,280 to own this property, covering the required deposit and purchase costs.

This is almost 25% of the purchase price and this is a key percentage that you need to remember when you are shopping for your property.

Once you have acquired the property you will be able to rent it out and therefore will have the benefit of the rental income and be responsible for the expenses.

You can see that the total ownership costs, including interest on the loan, come to A$30,249, so after collecting our rent of A$20,000 we have an annual cash holding cost of A$10,249.

This is how much we will need to find each year we own the property, assuming we do not reduce the loan.

We could pay an additional amount each year to reduce the loan, but the principal repayment would not be tax deductible, so may not be the most effective use of your cash.

We will look at the merits of reduction of debt in the next chapter.

It is important to note that if we have an annual holding cost, then the property must grow in value each year by at least this holding amount.

If not you will in fact be losing money on your investment, which is not our intention.

For this to occur, this property must grow by 2.56% p.a.

Most property should easily outperform this required growth amount, but make sure you do proper research so you feel confident this growth will be achieved.

If you do not feel this is likely, do not buy this property and keep looking for one you are more confident in.

This annual holding cost is funded by you and forms the basis of your tax position. Because it is a cost, this is fully tax deductible and ensures that you have no tax to pay.

In Australia, income tax is only levied on the net surplus, not the gross rental, so as there is indeed a loss; your income tax cost is zero.

This holding cost is then further increased by the tax incentives available to you such as travel and depreciation.

Depreciation is only available on new or near new property and is an entitlement rather than a cash cost. It first came into force in 1985, so if the property were acquired prior to that then no claim would exist.

Any renovations undertaken since 1985 would qualify.

No depreciation is not necessarily a bad thing as it is an incentive rather than requirement, however you will see that if it is available, it can have a very positive effect on your tax position.

If you have an old house, depreciation may be very low or nil so your tax loss would remain at the holding cost plus your travel costs if applicable.

If you acquired a new property, as in this case, you can see that your tax loss is increased substantially to A$22,255 p.a.

This is important as this amount will carry forward and continue to accrue over the years.

It will be available for you in the future to offset any annual rental surplus that the property may achieve, capital gains on sale or future Australian taxable income.

This may include salary or investment income on your eventual return to Australia. This is where it will be its most valuable.

Should you sell the property before returning to Australia (which is not necessary), then the accumulated loss is available to offset any capital gains tax.

In Australia there is no rate of Capital Gains Tax, rather the gain is added to your other income and taxed under the normal income tax rates.

There is an additional incentive that once you have owned the property longer than twelve months, then only half of any gain will be subject to taxation, the other half tax-free.

The twelve months relates to the contract signing dates, not actual settlements dates, so it is usually very easy to ensure the year has passed when property is concerned.

The taxable component of your gain is added to your other income, which in this case is a negative, and the combined amount is then taxed.

If the accumulated loss is equivalent to half of the total gain, then your combined taxable income will be nil and no tax will be payable on your capital gain.

As such, based on the example, the property could have grown in value by A$44,510 (twice the annual loss of A$22,255) before ant tax would be payable.

This equates to an annual growth rate based on the original cost of some 11.13% with no tax payable. Any growth above this level will attract some tax if this is your only property.

Had you had two or more properties, then the losses from each are pooled together and offset whichever gain is made.

It is important to note that the annual tax loss on the property does not belong to the property itself, it is allocated to the owners on a proportionate ownership basis.

Therefore one property's tax losses can be used on another property's capital gain. This is true even if the properties are in different states or cities within Australia.

As such the best way to ensure no tax at all is to have multiple property ownership building up tax credits to offset future capital profits.

Should you return to Australia, the accumulated tax credits will most likely be used to offset salary or retirement incomes. As such there may be some capital gains tax if you sell a few years after your return.

The amount will depend on your taxable income at the time, but in a worst case scenario, if you where on the top tax rate of 46.5% as a resident taxpayer, when this is applied to the half taxable component then an average capital gains tax of 23.25% on your full gain would be your tax cost.

Even at this level I am sure you would be very happy, as you may have recouped your accumulated tax losses at the 46.5% value against your salary so you are still well ahead.

You will never regret having too many tax losses carrying forward to protect against future income or capital gains tax.

In addition, the annual tax loss that you have will still be there to continue to reduce your salary tax each year. The only benefit you may lose is the claim for your travel of A$2,000 p.a. This reduces your annual tax loss to A$20,255 p.a.

Assuming you are now living in Australia, on a salary of say A$100,000 p.a., this tax loss would result in a tax reduction of A$8,406 p.a. which would come to you as a refund against your salary tax.

As you will recall, the actual holding cost of the property is only A$10,249 p.a. so your tax saving covers the bulk of the holding cost and it will only cost you A$1,843 p.a. to own the property from your own pocket.

Your foresight in acquiring the property while you were overseas when you could easily afford the holding costs, pays off handsomely as now the holding costs are basically funded through annual tax savings.

Had you not done this while overseas, it is unlikely that you could have afforded to start this investment once you are back in the Australian system. Again, remind yourself how it was when you were living in Australia prior to you becoming an expatriate.

Each property has different income and expense levels and you may find that your property may even be able to generate a surplus after the future tax benefits are taken into account.

You can plan your property portfolio to maximise this benefit simply by sensibly increasing your property ownership over time.

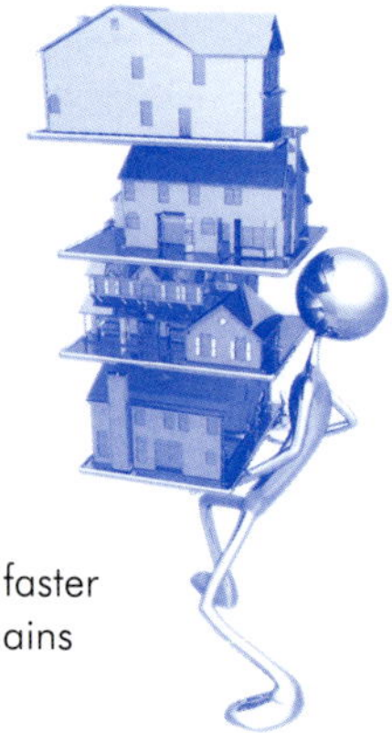

When you are looking to acquire your second property, you may wish to use some of the increased equity in your first to provide some of the deposit requirement.

This in essence means that you borrow more than 80% on the second purchase and preserves your cash for the important use of your residence when you return to Australia.

In doing so, you also build up your tax credits at a faster rate and provide additional protection for capital gains tax and future salary tax.

Your average debt level remains at no more than 80% (which is the most the banks will allow without Mortgage Insurance) but the borrowing amount is supported by the improving values of your property.

By sensibly monitoring your portfolio and savings power, you will easily achieve some outstanding results from both an investment and taxation perspective.

One warning though, do not be too greedy. Stay within your safe boundaries and seek the maximum profit on your investment properties.

These tax benefits are automatic as a result of your investment; they do not need to be contrived.

You should always seek the best property, highest rental and lowest holding cost.

I would rather you have more quality investment properties generating consistent growth and reasonable tax benefits than one slow growing property generating huge tax losses.

We are investors, not tax schemers.

With that attitude you can work wonders.

12. The Banks Are Your Best Friends

There is no doubt that the tax credits you build up through your property investment will be of significant benefit in ensuring your income tax is kept to a minimum and the opportunity for a tax free period when you return is maximised.

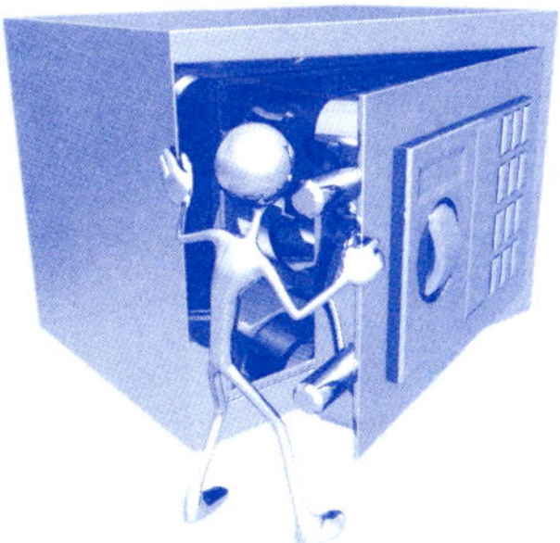

It is all well and good for me to recommend this course of action, after all I am a Tax Accountant, and it makes me look very good if you pay no tax.

But does the decision to borrow also improve the overall financial performance of your property investment.

I am going to show you that it will, in fact, have a large positive influence on your investment for a couple of reasons.

Investment Leveraging

Leveraging is an important and successful method of investment where you use other people's money (the banks) to assist with the purchase of assets.

The basis is that the growth and income will be in excess of the cost of borrowing leaving you with a profit overall.

This is enhanced when you acknowledge that you receive the growth on the total value of the asset, not withstanding that you have put in a smaller share of the purchase price.

Hopefully, the net return after deducting the cost of funds should be greater than if you had paid cash.

After Tax Return

Any legitimate tax savings made as a result of a prudent level of funding impact directly into your overall result.

Capital Gains Tax And Investment Return Analysis Over Five Years

	DEBT LEVEL	0%	50%	80%
Land, Building & Stamp Duty		416,000	416,000	416,000
Borrowing Expenses		0	2,280	2,280
Less Finance Amount		0	200,000	320,000
CLIENT CONTRIBUTION		416,000	218,280	98,280
Less: Income Received		66,675	0	0
Add: Income Tax levied		1,927	0	0
Add: Shortfall Funded		0	7,025	51,245
NET INVESTMENT		351,252	225,305	149,525
CAPITAL GAINS TAX LIABILITY				
Sale Price - Estimated Growth P.A.	7.00%	583,462	583,462	583,462
Less: Cost of House & Land		416,000	416,000	416,000
50% Exemption		83,731	83,731	83,731
Tax Losses Accrued		0	67,055	111,275
TAXABLE CAPITAL GAIN		83,731	16,676	-27,544
CAPITAL GAINS TAX		24,618	4,836	0
CASH POSITION ON SALE				
Sale Proceeds		583,462	583,462	583,462
Less: Tax Liability		24,618	4,836	0
Loan Repayment		0	200,000	320,000
NET FUNDS ON SALE		558,844	378,626	263,462
ANNUAL GROWTH ACHIEVED AFTER TAX		**8.87%**	**11.12%**	**14.67%**

If this can be proven, then the Banks may well be your best friends.

The second part of our Property Tax Estimator looks at this question and compares the overall return after all holding costs and taxation against three different borrowing levels.

We will use the same example as before of the A$400,000 property and perform an analysis over five years. I have also included an allowance of A$16,000 for purchase costs such as stamp duty & legals.

The first column assumes no borrowing so you pay the full amount of the purchase, the second assumes you borrow half of the purchase price and the third shows the effect of borrowing our recommended maximum of 80% of the purchase price.

You should always bear in mind, that the rental and growth performance of the property will not be impacted in any way regardless of how much or how little you borrow. The rent will be the same as will the growth.

What will change is how much of your money you contribute to purchase and keep the property.

The first significant difference is your Client Contribution, that's how much you need to put in at the start to take possession of the property.

Obviously with no loan the contribution from you is much higher, at A$416,000 compared to A$98,280 should you have fully financed the purchase.

The total purchase price is slightly higher when finance is undertaken as there are fees associated with the loan.

When you pay cash there is no interest cost so the rent will flow to you. Instead of having the annual deficit, you will now have a surplus after expenses of some A$66,675 in total over the five years.

You will note that the income tax on this amount is only A$1,927 in total. That seems absurd given Australia supposedly has very high tax rates.

It is in fact correct, as the tax effectiveness of the depreciation deductions comes true to reduce the income tax to a very small amount.

This is something important to remember as one day you could be looking for a tax effective retirement income.

The building depreciation lasts for 40 years so it will be there to help reduce your tax if you do pay the loan out when you need a retirement income.

General depreciation on the fittings does reduce over time but then will normally be refreshed every few years with renovation or refurbishment.

Do not underestimate the tax effectiveness of this source of income during your retirement.

On the face of it, the low income tax may seem good, however we have foregone our ability to carry forward losses in order to reduce the income tax and left ourselves exposed to Capital Gains Tax.

In any case, after deducting tax and rental return from your original contribution, your total net investment over the 5 years is A$351,252.

When a 50% loan is taken, there is a small surplus but importantly most of the depreciation benefits have been allowed to carry forward as the interest has done the bulk of the work in reducing the income tax liability.

The overall investment is reduced to A$225,305, substantially less than the option of paying cash.

With the full 80% loan, we are at our maximum benefit and minimum contribution level of A$149,525. You could have in fact bought two properties with the same amount of money, covering all costs.

This is good as it could spread your portfolio hopefully into two good areas or may be that you decide to buy a more valuable property in a better area, and fully exploit your buying power.

I have assumed that the property grows at 7% p.a. which may be conservative or optimistic depending on your view of the market.

You can produce this report on our websites and substitute any other growth level you wish to consider based upon your research and expectations.

I believe that 7% p.a. is a fair level, on average, to predict and in any case this example is only to demonstrate the merit of borrowing rather than predict the performance of property.

You should recall that the breakeven point is where your property recovers the cash holding cost through growth.

Moving on, when we sell the property at the 7% growth rate, we would achieve a sale price of A$583,462, which is the same in each case.

Because we have owned the property more than twelve months, half of the gain is capital gains tax free and we are also allowed to deduct off the accumulated Tax Credits built up.

That is where the main difference occurs. With the no loan purchase we have used our tax credits to reduce the income tax so we are left with a Capital Gains Tax bill of A$24,618, whereas with the full loan we have the losses assisting us to have a nil Capital Gains tax position.

Once we pay off the loan and any tax from the sale proceeds we are left with the net after tax proceeds of A$558,844, A$378,626 and A$263,462 respectively.

However, when we work out the rate of return on the money you have actually put in initially and subsequent to purchase, the rates of return strongly support the argument to finance the purchase.

When no borrowing is undertaken, the after tax return is 8.87% p.a.

Whereas, when we borrow the maximum, the after tax annual return is increased to 14.67%, which includes deducting all costs including interest.

This is almost double the rate of return achieved when paying cash on the same investment, and is a compelling argument to befriend the bank.

This analysis assumes that you sell whilst you are overseas.

It is impossible to calculate the benefit once you return, but safe to say that the combined effect of the leveraging and the fact that the annual deduction can be converted to cash when you are back in Australia would only enhance this position.

Using finance will not only reduce your tax, but will also improve your return.

One other important aspect of acting besides the obvious tax advantages and investment performance, is in the fact that you acquire the property at today's price rather than tomorrows.

If you choose to continue to delay your decision to invest, then the price just keeps rising, so you inevitably just pay more for the same property later on.

I do not want you to rush out and get into a debt burden that you cannot afford, but you should always look at sensibly having some debt in each purchase.

If you already have a property that you have paid off, do not worry.

Being debt free is never a bad thing, especially if you are living in the property. Look at it as simply maximising the performance of the property asset.

What you have to consider always is average portfolio debt.

If one property is debt free it can be used to allow another to be purchased with 100% debt, which may mean the average over both properties is now 50%.

So if you have available equity, strongly consider using it to help improve your overall portfolio returns.

One day, you will want to pay off the bank.

That is normally only when one of three things happen.

- **You sell the property**, so logically should pay it off.
- **You have surplus cash and want a tax effective income stream**, only at the time you need the income.
- **You move into the house as your future residence**, and therefore the interest is no longer tax deductible.

Otherwise you should resist early repayment and retain your cash for your dream home when you return.

13. Let Time Be On Your Side

One of the only negatives about this tax planning method is that it is not a quick fix.

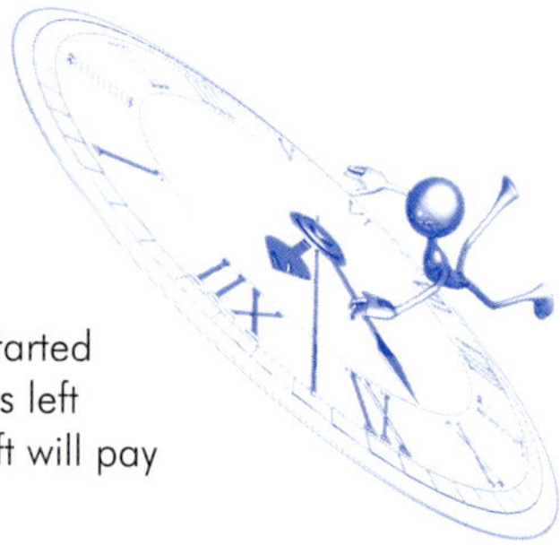

Building a quality investment portfolio, accruing your tax credits and achieving your savings goals need as much time as you can give.

If you are fortunate enough to have just started you expatriate life, or still have many years left overseas, then using the time you have left will pay handsome dividends.

Consider the following table:

Approximate Cost To Acquire (25%)	A$ 98,200
Annual Holding Cost Per Property	A$ 10,249
Annual Rental Loss	A$ 22,255
Effect Of Time	
Accumulated Tax Losses	
After 5 Years	A$ 111,275
After 10 Years	A$ 222,550
Effect Of Multiple Ownership	
Accumulated Tax Losses	
Two Properties – 5 Years	A$ 222,550
Three Properties – 5 Years	A$ 333,825
Three Properties – 10 Years	A$ 667,650

The effect of time and multiple ownerships can quickly propel you to significant tax savings opportunity.

As mentioned, these Accumulated Tax Losses can offset the capital gain on your property at effectively a two for one rate due to the 50% exemption on capital gains tax.

Alternatively they can offset a considerable sum of future Australian taxable income, ensuring a lengthy tax-free period on a salary or almost assuring you of a tax-free retirement when you return to Australia.

When you also consider the actual cash cost of the tax credits used in this example it is even more attractive.

At A$10,249 per property per year, the cash cost of building 10 years of losses totalling A$222,550, is only A$102,490.

When the tax credits are potentially worth up to 46.5% this is undoubtedly the safest, and most sensible way to build a strong legitimate Australian tax position.

All is not lost if you are going home soon, do as much as you can within the realms of investment safety and time still available to you.

You may never get this opportunity again when you return to Australia, especially as you will most likely be generating a salary and will loose the advantage of accumulating the annual deficit, as it will be used to reduce the yearly tax on your salary

Tax planning takes time to achieve the best results, start as soon as you can.

Your buying power should be put to best use as the effect of multiple ownerships also dramatically improves your position.

You may not be able to extend the time left for your expatriate life, but you could enhance your build up by owning more properties or acquiring more expensive property.

Remember our example is based on just one A$400,000 property.

I am very sure we can all find quality investment property at a higher value, which will improve our tax credit accrual.

You can see from acquiring three properties of this value and staying abroad for 10 years, you could return to Australia with A$667,650 of accumulated tax credits.

If your salary was A$100,000 p.a. on return it would be over 6 years before you had to pay any income tax.

Alternatively, you could sell all the properties and make a A$1.3 million capital gain and use the tax credits to offset the capital gains tax in full on this amount, leaving the funds clear to acquire or payout your family home and be debt free.

It is hard to predict the future, but at least you have a choice as to what the future will be.

It is, however, impossible to change the past. Once your time abroad has elapsed there is no going back to alter what you could or should have done.

If you take full advantage of these circumstances and build a quality portfolio with sensible debt levels and you will never regret the time abroad and can enjoy many years of tax free living in Australia as well as the satisfaction of significant quality property assets.

14. And Now My Castle

One of the most common questions asked of me by expatriates is "should I buy my future home whilst overseas?"

Very simply the answer is yes.

The improvement in your buying power alone makes it very sensible to acquire your eventual home during your time abroad, but importantly you should treat it as an investment property until you do actually return to Australia.

This is also true if you already had a home when you left Australia.

This is also true when you consider that the most important fact is to be debt free on your home when living in Australia.

It is hard enough to save the amount for the property at today's prices but even harder if you leave it for later.

On average Australian property doubles every 7 years, so a house that you are looking to live in worth say A$800,000 today is likely to be A$1,600,000 in 7 years.

If you buy it now, not only do you gain the tax advantages, but you also lock in the price and your savings target.

Premium property also has a tendency to outperform the general market, so you may find the decision to be an astute one from an investment perspective as well.

The problem you may face is that during your time overseas, your views and circumstances may change dramatically and what today is definitely your home, tomorrow may not be as appropriate as you initially thought.

This change of intent may have nothing to do with the property itself, but could be influenced by such factors as,

- You can now afford a better option,
- You could get relocated to another Australian city on return for career or lifestyle reasons,
- You may now have a larger family and need a bigger property,
- Your tastes have simply changed from the overseas influences you were exposed to.

All of these things can and do occur, but are not a negative.

It is also difficult, due to distance and time constraints, to actually find your dream home while you are overseas.

In fact, I believe that to find your eventual home while abroad is something that requires a lot of luck.

What is important is to ensure your strategy can accommodate a change in direction should it occur.

You should never loose sight of the importance of being debt free on your eventual residence in Australia. It is one of the most critical issues when you return.

If there is a remote likelihood that the home you have today may not be your home tomorrow, the simplest way to accommodate this possibility is to leave the mortgage at its highest level until you actually move in.

Therefore we always recommend that you refrain from making additional repayments on any of your properties, and instead retain cash or other liquid investments so that when you return to Australia, so you can objectively make a decision as to which property will now be your home, and then apply the cash towards that.

This works regardless of whether you were lucky enough to have bought it prior or if you are now on the hunt for that perfect house.

Buying your future residence while living abroad, is a decision you will never regret.

The best thing about buying what I will call a potential home whilst abroad, is that you have now set a "static target" for your savings plan.

You have acquired the property at today's value and have a clear knowledge as to how much you need to put away to pay off the mortgage when you eventually return, but not before.

If you do not manage to find a potential home while you are away, which is very common, then you have a "moving target" as you do not know how much you will need to purchase the property at some future date.

This makes planning somewhat harder, particularly if the areas you would like to live in perform well and keep growing in value.

This would encourage you to be more disciplined with your savings and look closely at building up a property portfolio so that you are at least keeping pace with the rises in the property market.

Many people wrongly believe that the tax-free status of your Australian "principal place of residence" will apply to a home you buy while overseas.

This is not true as for the exemption to apply you must be a "Tax Resident" when you acquire the property and live in it.

It will only become tax free from the time you actually take up residence on your return to Australia on a pro rata basis.

In summary, if you can find your "castle" while abroad or were lucky enough to have it already, then still employ the strategy of considering it as an investment property and reduce the debt only when you move in on a permanent basis and are convinced it will be your long-term residence.

15. Leave Out The Lemons

What we have been working through is how to build a property portfolio by exploiting the advantages of the tax system while you are an expatriate.

This system works fantastically but is dependant upon the property growing in value and the growth out pacing your annual cash holding costs.

I will once again remind you that you are an investor first and foremost, so our prime objective is to seek the best growth property we can.

I have done well personally from property and watched many of my clients do even better.

The tax benefits are the same for high and low performing property, so you might as well buy the best property you can.

From my observations I have discovered that there is no perfect property, they are all good if you ride out cycles and hold for the long term, but there are some simple rules to follow if you want to give yourself the best chance of above average success.

Location

We always hear people talk about "Location, Location, Location" when it comes to property, but they rarely define what is a good location.

My observations have led me to believe that this means closeness to amenities, such as schools, transport and lifestyle amenities such as shops and entertainment.

These all count strongly to a good location.

What makes a brilliant location though, is closeness to two important things, a water body and the City.

The closer you are to both the better.

As humans we seem to have a natural affinity to water so these areas can almost assuredly guarantee above average performance any where in the world. If you can get a view of the water, even better.

The City is "life". We are drawn to it; it offers all that we want from jobs to entertainment. It is not surprising that we like to be near it.

Quality Always

Long-term success as a property investor is decided at purchase. As such when you buy, find the best quality you can.

Quality in construction, finish, design and attributes.

It is safer to pay a higher price today for a better property than to try and rectify issues later.

Follow the Money

Identifying where the money is flowing is one of the most critical aspects of property investment.

There are two different types of money flow to look for.

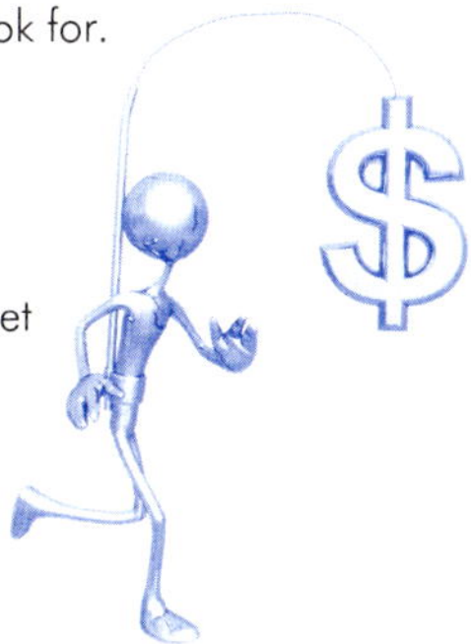

Lifestyle Flow

As I mentioned earlier, I have never won a financial argument over lifestyle. I could be upset about this or learn to use it as an advantage.

It is a fact that people will pay more for a lifestyle asset than a financial one, so why not exploit this to your advantage.

In areas where the lifestyle is very good, you will normally achieve better than average gains. This may be a select suburb, magnificent apartment block or coastal retreat.

Whatever the type does not matter. What does is that you identify the lifestyle benefits of your purchase.

Development Flow

There are still some less desirable suburbs around Australia that have good fundamentals such as location but may be in need of regeneration.

Once developers start entering these areas, substantial improvement in quality and value usually follows.

Development can make everything better so if you think you can spot an area where developers may come one day, then it is certainly worth the wait.

Why is it a Bargain?

If you are offered a bargain, you must dig deeper and be sure it is in fact a bargain.

We all love a bargain and they do exist. Sometimes they are lemons coated in sugar, so be careful.

These days it is harder to find one but be sure it is. It may be that the property is available as a result of the current owner's hardship or it needs some money spent on it.

I recommend you always consider a bargain when it is presented, but only proceed if you can clearly identify reasons why it is a bargain.

If you can't then is it really a bargain?

Would You Live in It?

Such an obvious question, but an important one.

Given that you are going to be a landlord, someone has to pay you rent and for that to occur the property must be "liveable".

If you would be reluctant to live in the property, for whatever reason, then why would anyone else?

This is particularly true if you want to see increasing rent over your period of ownership.

Would You Pay Yourself A Profit?

Can you foresee that in the future this property could be sold for a profit?

We all know that property has always grown over time, but the better growth can be seen at the time of purchase.

This is where you process the information on location and lifestyle attributes and try and generate an answer to the pressing question, will it grow in value?

If you cannot see that it is going to be more valuable tomorrow, then keep looking, this one is not for you.

Local Ownership Rate

Areas where there is a high owner-occupier rate will generally out perform.

The exception to this rule is first home areas. This is because these are that I would call "stepping stone zones", where people buy there as a matter of affordability until they can sell and move into other more desirable areas.

Apart from those areas, which still offer profit potential if the other positive attributes are present, look for suburbs where people want to live in as owners.

This normally means higher demand and lower supply helping you achieve better growth and rental.

Renovate for Profit

A lot of people under estimate the value of renovation.

Not only will it usually give you an immediate boost to the value of the property over and above the money spent, but it will also mean an increased rental.

If you have a good property that is looking a bit jaded, do the maths on a reasonable renovation and you might be pleasantly surprised at the result.

Be careful to not go overboard and spend your budget wisely. Also be mindful as to what you want to do after renovation, sell or rent?

You may be far more generous on a renovation done for resale rather then just a tidy up for rental.

Respect the Tenant

As an investor, a good tenant is critical for you to have a hassle free property investment.

Many people under value their tenant to their own detriment. Remember, they are not just paying you rent, but looking after your valuable property.

I would always recommend that you look after the requirements of a good tenant and be reasonable on rent increases.

The rental market in Australia is basically safe everywhere, particularly on new and premium property.

Australian property has always been geared towards achieving growth rather than high rents. As long as you are receiving a fair market value and solid annual growth you should be happy.

If the tenant takes good care of your property he should be rewarded with stable rental.

A good rental agent is also very important and you should make sure that who ever is looking after your property is doing their best to ensure a quality tenant is located and maintained in your property.

There are many rental agents in all areas of Australia so you can be selective and make sure that they have your best interests at heart.

Buy the Best You Can Afford

With the advantage of improved buying power while you remain an expatriate, you should fully exploit the opportunity.

Always buy the best you can afford as there is safety in owning quality. It may mean a better suburb, bigger house or more impressive view.

For example in an apartment block, there is an increase in prices for the higher floors with the better outlooks. These may not be much more expensive (particularly as you are financing them and putting a minimum deposit down) but the extra view will make it a lot easier to sell the apartment at a premium in the future.

Own Use Value

If there is a chance that you may make use of the property in the future, then you may wish to be more generous on the price than you otherwise would.

A beach house may be a future holiday home so you have the opportunity to acquire it in today's dollars rather than a higher price at a later date.

This is true for a wide range of property that you may wish to have in your portfolio, such as potential retirement homes.

You may well be prepared to receive a lower rental return in the short term as the future personal benefit may compensate for this.

It is impossible to quantify a future personal benefit, only you can balance it up based on your goals and expectations.

Individuality

Australian property is very diverse in style, type, location and usage. I believe you need to look at each on its own merit, as it is very much an individual market rather than a group market.

That is two houses on the same street will not necessarily perform equally. One may do substantially better than the other because of some individual characteristics.

This may be block size, rezoning ability, house style, view or some other attribute.

Make sure you look for the key positive attributes of your purchase. The more positives, the higher the likelihood of improved returns.

Let Time Be on Your Side

Every property on the planet has risen in value over the last 30 years.

I do not make this statement foolishly to blank out the risk of property investment, however I am sure that in the future all property will continue to rise.

Where you can loose money is by selling it at the wrong time.

I am a great believer in holding property for as long as possible for the most gains.

Normally when the media is pushing the negative message, it is a good time to buy rather than sell.

The longer you can hold, the happier you will be.

The Australian property market has a historic trend that usually sees a few years of low property value growth, followed by a few years of moderate growth, then one or two years of strong growth. That then brings it back to the start of the cycle and it begins once again.

This is commonly referred to as a Cycle, with each period of differing growth called a phase.

Australian property markets generally follow a 7-year cycle, with each capital city having the same trend but with differing time stages.

One city may be booming at the same time another is stagnant, but they will still follow the same path eventually.

You can seek out as many statistics as you wish from the Real Estate Institute and promoting developers and make your own judgement.

This trend supports a long-term hold strategy as we can benefit from the consistent growth performance.

Avoid Speculation

The Australian property market is not an ideal one in which to speculate for quick returns. It is possible to make short-term profits but not common.

One of the reasons for this is that the entry costs (stamp duty) and exit costs (selling commissions) are quite high. These can be around 2-5% each way.

This may mean that you have to increase the value almost 10% just to cover the costs of the transaction, a task not easily achieved.

These costs can be easily recovered over the long term, and obviously the longer the better.

Another factor is of course taxation. You will recall that a 50% exemption on Capital Gains Tax applies if the asset has been owned longer than twelve months.

If you speculate and sell in less than a year, then the entire profit is subject to tax and could result in a reasonable portion of your profit being donated to the government.

These guidelines should see you with a successful investment.

If you delve in to the historical performance of Australian property, you will find that there is a strong consistency between the performance of all states and all types of property.

We maintain a significant amount of information on our website at **www.aussieproperty.com** and I would invite you to visit it to keep up to date with critical information affecting you as an investor and to keep abreast of the latest market performance statistics.

We also have more detailed reports on specific topics such as Property Cycles and Growth Drivers which you may enjoy at your leisure.

You can feel safe in buying Australian property and by ticking off this checklist hopefully achieve a better than average result, and because you have followed our tax planning strategies, at a low or no tax cost on your returns.

16. State Of Affairs

We have worked through the income and capital gains tax issues as an expatriate and shown you the benefits of owning Australian property during your time as an expatriate.

There are some state taxes that will also impact on you as a property investor that you should be aware of.

Unfortunately, these taxes cannot be reduced in any way as they relate to the ownership of the asset and there is no way to reduce them.

Each state has different tax rates and rules so you need to check each depending where you intend to purchase.

Federal tax issues aren't the only ones to consider. The State's have some duties that affect property ownership as well.

Stamp Duty

Stamp Duty is a state government charge levied on the contract of purchase of any property.

It is levied on the purchase price and normally increases as the purchase price also rises.

On average the stamp duty will be in a range of 3-6% of the purchase price, so it does add a reasonable amount to your entry cost.

You can offset the cost of Stamp Duty against your Capital Gains Tax when the property is eventually sold.

You should note that the banks will not finance this stamp duty in the purchase price so you will need to ensure that you have sufficient funds available to meet this cost when you acquire your property.

Each State also offers various concessions on Stamp Duty and also some cash incentives for First Home Buyers.

Unfortunately these may not be available to you if you are living overseas, as most will require you to live in the property within the first year of purchase.

Being overseas and the financial benefits that brings, would normally mean that the First Home Buyer concessions do not warrant returning to Australia to obtain.

If you happen to be returning to Australia soon, and have not yet owned any Australian property, then you may be able to take advantage of these programs.

There are two ways that you may be able to keep stamp duty to a minimum.

House & Land

If you are buying a plot of land and then building a house upon it, the stamp duty is significantly reduced if the land and building are on separate contracts.

This is because stamp duty will only be levied upon the land contract and not the separate building contract.

It is important that you keep these two apart wherever possible, as combining them will mean that stamp duty is levied upon the total value.

Victoria Off The Plan

Buying off the plan in Victoria offers the incentive where stamp duty is levied on the value if the property at the time of signing.

This can result in stamp duty savings of many thousands of dollars.

When you sign your purchase contract before the building

construction has commenced, you are charged stamp duty on the land value of the contract.

As construction begins, then the stamp duty is levied on a progressive basis to reflect the completed stages until eventually the stamp duty is charged in full once construction is completed.

This is a major incentive from the Victoria government to encourage investment towards new projects, and unfortunately is not available in any other state.

Land Tax

Each state levies an annual levy based on an assessed value of the property.

In all cases, property that is used for your personal residence is exempt from Land Tax, only property rented or vacant are subject to tax.

This value may not reflect the true market value, as most use an "unimproved value" to calculate the land tax component.

All states offer a tax-free threshold which will normally mean that you can own at least one property and still be under the land tax radar.

All properties owned in the same name are grouped and then the tax rate applies.

Land tax is normally a very small cost against your rental unless your portfolio is quite valuable.

It is fully tax deductible against your income tax each year.

As Land Tax is levied upon the amalgamated value of all your properties, it can be somewhat of a detriment to acquiring many properties as the cost can escalate with multiple property ownership.

This is also true as it cannot be recovered from your residential tenant through increased rental, so it becomes an owner's cost and can impact your cash flow.

Once you start to have a portfolio that is incurring Land tax, you may wish to consider acquiring property in other states. In doing this you will benefit from the tax-free allowance in each state.

NSW Vendor Tax

In 2004 The NSW State Government introduced a Vendor Tax which was levied when a property was sold for more than 12% of its original purchase price.

This Vendor Tax was 2.25% of the sale price and was a major factor in the NSW property market slowing greatly between 2004 and 2006.

Thankfully this Vendor Tax was removed in August 2005 and no longer operates, so you do not have to be concerned about it anymore.

This failed experiment should ensure that no such tax will ever be introduced in any Australian state.

These levies should not be a deterrent to investing in quality Australian property as they are just a by-product of being a successful property investor.

They do need to be carefully considered as they can have an impact on your purchase budget and annual holding costs, so make sure you make due enquiry prior to signing off on your purchase contract.

17. GST & Property

We have concentrated on the income and capital gains tax issues of your property investment in Australia and seen that it is in fact very advantageous to use property as your primary tax-planning tool.

The other tax operating in Australia is a Goods & Services Tax (GST) and it does have some impact on your property purchase and ownership.

GST was introduced on the 1st July 2000 and has had a very positive impact on the Australian economy. Despite initial negative media, GST has now well and truly been absorbed into the normal life of every Australian.

Even though most people living in Australia would probably complain about GST (just because it is a tax) it has helped the Australian business economy by removing many previously imposed taxes and increasing the need for financial discipline that is necessary in business success.

A full GST Refund is available for Australian landlords living out of Australia between 1st July 2000 and 31st March 2005.

The GST is currently levied at 10% on the supply of all goods and services in Australia by business. The current rate is supposedly entrenched in legislation. For it to change all State Parliaments must agree at the same time.

I will leave you to be the judge as to the likelihood of that.

You should note that even though the GST is collected by the Federal Government, the proceeds are passed on to the states, so each state directly benefits from additional activity in their economy.

Regardless of your ideology in regard to such a tax, it has helped the Australian economy remain as one of the world's most stable throughout the chaos that has tested many larger countries.

When it comes to property, the effects of GST are most felt when a new purchase is made.

This is because the 10% GST must be charged by the developer.

You will find that all prices you are quoted for property will be inclusive of GST. Legally this is the case unless otherwise stated, so do not worry that it will be in additional amount

I did many seminars on the introduction of the GST and bravely predicted that it would be a positive for the property market and be quickly absorbed into the system.

This has in fact occurred, and in reality I see the GST as the main insurance to protect the future of the tax advantages of property.

If you consider that the Government receives approximately 7-8% of the purchase price of new property as a tax collection, you can see that there is significant financial incentive to attract and encourage you towards ongoing investment in new property.

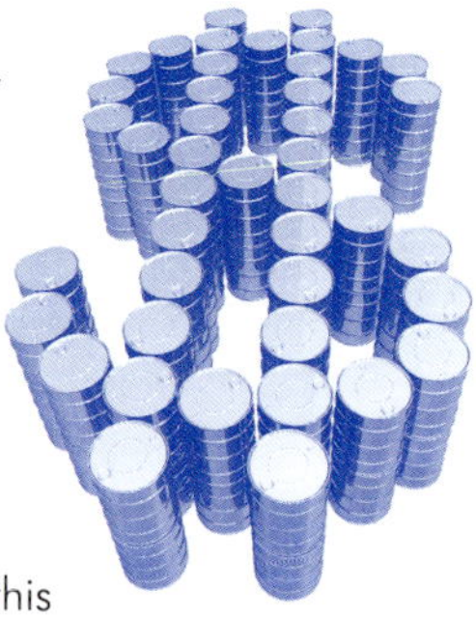

If you are buying a new property, look for areas where some of the GST collection is being spent on improved infrastructure such as schools, roads or community facilities. It is very likely that this spending will improve your growth prospects over time.

GST is a business tax, it is only charged by people carrying on a business in Australia, hence why it is payable when a property is purchased from someone in the business of development.

If you acquire a pre-owned residential property from an individual non-developer, then no GST is payable.

In the same way, when you sell your property in the future, you will not have to charge GST as you are not in the "business" of property, merely an investor.

The rent you collect on your property is also excluded from the GST system if it is a residential tenancy. Your holding costs will have some GST included, but this is very negligible and will not be noticeable to you.

A recent ruling now allows overseas-based landlords to get no GST paid on property expenses.

It applies only for the period 1st July 2000 to 31st March 2005, after this date the rules where changed to confirm that GST is payable on all property expenses.

If you have paid GST during this period you may be entitled to obtain a refund of the amounts paid form your property manager or service provider. The refund cannot be claimed from the Tax Office, only the person who originally collected it from you.

To qualify for the GST refund you must have been living overseas at the time, and not been required to register for GST (which means you did not have business operations).

You can claim a refund on all operational costs of the property and services that relate to the activity of being a landlord.

This includes:

- Property Management Services
- Body Corporate Services
- Property Maintenance (but not replacement of items)
- Property Buyers Fees
- Legal Fees
- Accounting Fees

We do have a GST Refund Kit on our ***www.smats.net*** website to assist you with this should you require.

Commercial rents under A$50,000 p.a. are also excluded, but GST may be payable when rents exceed this amount. There will also be issues in regard to GST on sale, which you will need to seek professional advice upon.

Safe to say that GST will have an invisible effect on your property investment in Australia, and will work behind the scenes to keep the economy as stable as possible for you to enjoy a safe market environment.

18. Where To Now?

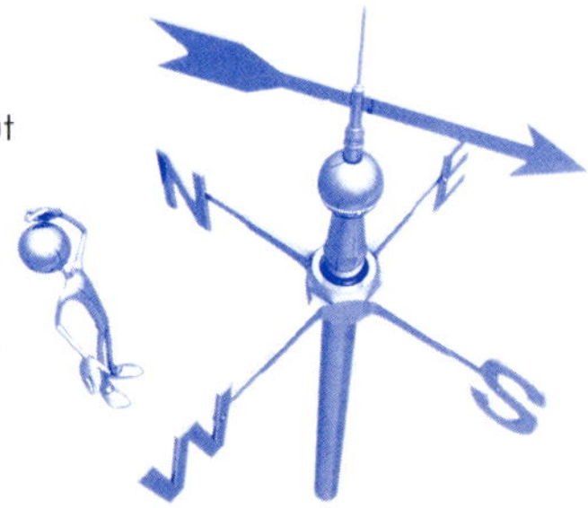

I am sure by now you are ready to go out and find that quality Australian property to get your tax planning underway.

Being overseas, it is not always that easy to find them given the distance and time constraints you face as an expatriate.

To help you get going, here is a summary of some of the purchasing options available to you.

Finding your property is often the hardest part. The finance, tax and ownership issues are easy after that.

Selling Agents

There are many professional selling agents operating throughout the world offering Australian property.

You want to make sure that they offer the property at the same prices as offered in Australia, as sometimes there may be a marketing premium. This does not normally occur with larger, well-established agents, but it always pays to check.

You should also ensure that they offer you the level of service and information that you need as an overseas-based investor, which due to their level of experience should be readily available.

Buyers Agents

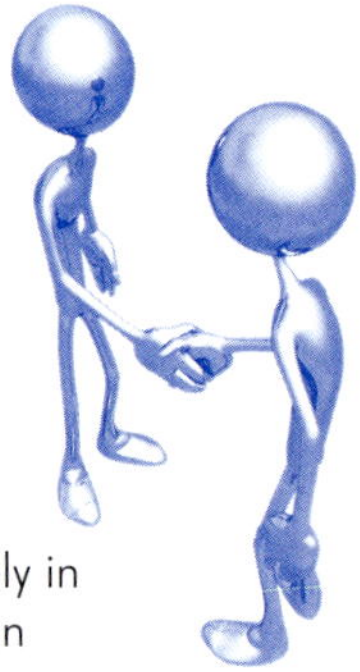

A relatively new phenomenon in Australia is the Buyers Agent.

These are well-qualified real estate agents that have moved away from the traditional selling role to now be acting for the buyer. They charge a fee for the service but act purely in your interests to find, present and negotiate an attractive purchase price for you.

This trend is particularly popular in New South Wales and Victoria where the property values and scarcity have supported the need for an agent to assist you find an appropriate property.

Normally you would expect the cost to be far less than the benefit of convenience, negotiated discount and improved selection through the network of a buying agent.

The Property Buyers Agents Association of Australia website can be found at *www.pbaaa.com.au*.

Developer Direct

Many developers regularly promote their properties overseas. You may even find some that have offices overseas in your location.

Depending on market conditions, developers are sometimes keen to offer incentives to prospective purchasers and can offer you a selection of a number of different projects.

As long as they offer property that fits into the selection criteria we have discussed, this can be a very attractive method of purchase as normally the property will be brand new and offer the maximum depreciation allowances.

Internet

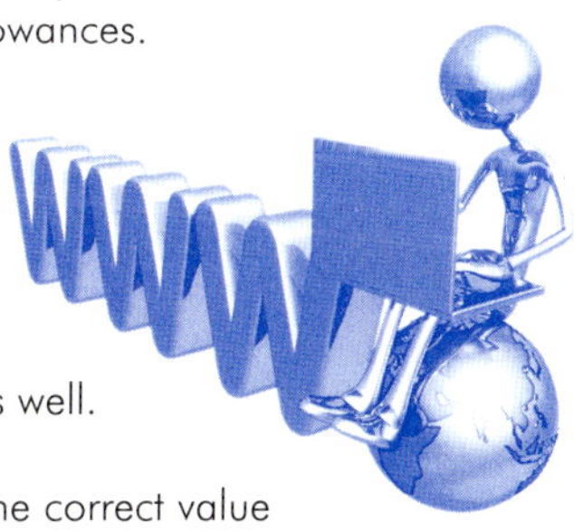

As with most things these days, the Internet offers a wide array of information. This is true of Australian property as well.

It is not always easy to judge the correct value on Internet promoted property but it is always a good location to research availability and gauge price levels for the property you are looking at.

Most developers and agents will also offer a great deal of

information on the Internet so it is always worth a look.

I have recently launched our own website dedicated to the specific needs of offshore based Australian property investors at *www.aussieproperty.com*.

It is full of information and is sponsored by some of the leading property companies in Australia.

It is not for profit site and I do not receive any commissions from anyone in order to ensure the integrity of the site.

It is a member site, so you will be required to register in order to gain access to all the critical information and tool areas of the site.

As you have taken the time to read my book I would like to extend to you a free upgrade to "Gold Member" status. When you register, use the promotional code "XPBOOK" and this will automatically ensure your elevated status on the site with various special member benefits including rebates and discounts.

This is also where you can keep up to date with the Australian property market and expand your knowledge base.

There are some expanded topics on property investing issues as well as the latest market statistics.

Buying Visits

If you have the time, then there is nothing like shopping for property.

Even if you cannot find something in the time available, it will give you a good look at the options available.

Alternatively you can do your pre-arrival communication with the agents or developers and then a pre purchase inspection to confirm your acquisition.

There is nothing like seeing something before buying, however given time is a factor and most good property may not wait for your arrival, it is not an essential aspect when purchasing.

Family & Friends

Many of our clients call upon the favour of family and friends to either assist in locating a property or confirming that they should proceed with the purchase.

As long as they have an understanding of the scope of your purchasing power and have some knowledge of the general market conditions, this can be very helpful.

I have found that sometimes they can be clouded by their own circumstances, which will be very different to yours now that you are an expatriate, but that can be a balancing argument to ensure you are comfortable prior to proceeding.

Whichever method you choose to use in purchasing your property will depend on your personal circumstances and preferences.

We all have differing budgets and tastes, so what appeals to one person may be completely inappropriate to another.

One of the most important aspects of overseas ownership is mental comfort.

You need to be happy with your purchase, so do not be afraid to ask questions, research and properly assess all aspects before committing.

Liking your property is almost as important as choosing the right investment fundamentals.

It is very probable that you will own your property for many years, so the more it appeals to you the better.

19. Defusing The Foreign Currency Question

When you are working abroad, another confusing option available to you is in which currency is best to finance in.

You may well have the option to borrow in the currency of your earnings when acquiring an Australian property.

On the face of it, the Australian dollar interest rate can appear expensive compared to some other currencies, but this is not what you should make your decision upon.

In the below table, we compare a USD loan at 5% p.a. interest against an AUD loan of 7.3%

Based on Exchange at start of USD/AUD 75c	If Australian Dollar Weakens	If the Dollar Remains Unchanged	If Australian Dollar Strengthens
Estimated Value in 12 months	70c	75c	80c
Interest Rate USD Loan	5.0%	5.0%	5.0%
Effect of Currency Movement as an annual %	6.7%	0.0%	-6.7%
Total Effective Interest Cost	11.7%	5.0%	-1.7%
Australian Interest Rate	7.3%	7.3%	7.3%
Additional Cost/(Benefit) of Australian Dollar Loan	(4.4%)	2.3%	9.0%
Best Currency Based on projected Currency Value	AUD	USD	USD

One would logically assume that the USD loan was cheaper as the interest was at a lower rate, however this is only the case if the currency does not erode by more than the interest differential.

You can see from the table that if the Australian dollar weakens during the loan period, then the "higher" interest rate is actually cheaper as no currency exchange cost would have been incurred.

Alternatively, had the Australian dollar strengthened during the loan period, not only have you benefited from a lower interest rate, but the currency gain has in essence covered the cost of the loan creating a double benefit.

Timing and luck is an important element in getting things right here, but you can reduce the risks by following these three simple rules when you want to explore the option of foreign currency lending.

Australian Dollar Borrowing has NO RISK

First and foremost, you must realise that when you borrow in Australian dollars, you have no currency risk at all because you have borrowed in the currency of the asset.

Therefore no matter what happens to the currency you will always maintain your Australian dollar equity. In essence it is a full currency hedge against any movement.

What you do lose is opportunity. One to make gains on the currency and another to potentially save on the interest cost.

In reality this lost opportunity is not as significant as it seems, as the risks you inherit may be great.

I must confess that I believe that there are enough risks associated with investments and general expatriate life without deliberately bringing in additional ones.

In the main, the cost of Australian dollar borrowing is equity insurance and comes with the guarantee of maintaining your wealth and of a full tax deduction for your interest cost.

In addition, borrowing in Australian dollars offers the maximum loan, so if you are deposit sensitive, then it will be your only initial option. This is because financiers will reduce their lending rate on foreign currency loans to protect their security position in case the currency shifts.

They will normally require you to put in additional 5-10% equity into the purchase to cover any potential currency loss from your larger equity position rather than having to make a margin call.

That is not to say that it would be necessary to do so, but we are increasingly reminded that anything can happen in this world we live in.

But there have been times when the opportunity is sufficiently large enough to warrant some risk.

Always Borrow in the Currency Most Likely To Weaken

The second rule is the most important if you choose to take a multi currency loan.

You must note that you should never take a foreign currency loan that does not allow you to switch between the foreign currencies. If this facility is not available do not take the loan, as if you get caught on the wrong side of a currency slide, the financial losses can be catastrophic.

The difficulty is in determining which currency is most likely to weaken.

I would like to introduce you to the concept of "Natural Range".

That is the trading band that a currency moves over in normal circumstances. Currency is a traded commodity that will usually range over a band as markets react to information.

We all have a different opinion of what the natural range might be. I normally ask my clients, "What would you be happy to convert money to Australian dollars at?". Normally when you are content to convert, that is what you consider to be the natural range.

When the currency is outside of the perceived natural range, then risk and opportunity are created.

This can be further complicated by the fact that the natural range may move over time thus making it hard to properly assess if we are outside the natural range or if in fact the range has moved.

Once you establish what you consider to be a natural range at least you have a starting point to assess the merit of Foreign Currency lending.

It is fair to say, that the Australian dollar interest rate is higher than most other currencies. You need to understand the important issue of face value rate. Simply, when we are comparing interest rates we are dealing with apples and oranges, as the currencies are very different.

In a general sense, the difference between the quoted Australian dollar rate and that of another currency, is the implied currency risk. In theory, the wider the gap between the two rates, the higher the risk.

In the example, the Australian rate is 7.3% p.a. and the US rate is 5% p.a., therefore there is an implied risk of 2.3% p.a. that the US currency will strengthen against the Australian dollar over the year.

As long as the US currency does not strengthen by any more than 2.3% you will have a benefit. If it strengthens more than 2.3% you will have lost out and be eroding your equity.

The thing you have to be most careful about is that this

currency movement is based on 2.3% p.a.

Currency is highly volatile and can easily move this much in one month. If it did, then the annualised movement would be the equivalent of paying 27.6%pa interest.

I am sure you will agree that in that case it would have been much better to have borrowed in Australian dollars at a fixed total cost of 7.3%pa.

Hence you should be careful to not get too drawn by the face value rate, and must assess what the total impact is including what affect currency movement may also have.

The only time you should borrow in a foreign currency is if you believe that the Australian dollar will strengthen in the foreseeable future or if you believe that the Australian dollar will weaken by less than the interest differential.

The strengthening currency does not come as a cost to you but forms an additional amount outstanding should you wish to convert back to Australian dollars to repay the debt from sale proceeds.

On the other hand if you had the good fortune to pick the currency most likely to weaken, this movement would be in your favour as your loan would be decreasing and when you convert back to Australian dollars you would in fact owe less than before.

This can be further boosted by the lower face value interest rate that you have had along the way.

Following the key rules of Multi Currency lending and passive monitoring of the currency markets can be very rewarding.

Importantly, you should also note that any currency losse cannot be claimed as an expense against your Australian income tax and that any gains would not be subject to tax.

This is why you have to be very sure as to your expectations of where you think the currency will be in the future.

Many clients are prepared to assume this risk as they can use their foreign currency salary to fund the repayments and this serves as a safety position whilst you are abroad.

Take Your Profits

If you have had the good luck and wisdom to pick the currency most likely to weaken and are receiving the benefit thereon, your next dilemma is when to switch back.

You should try and switch from one currency to the other at, or near, the end of movement cycles.

In many ways it is like being on a winning streak at the casino. Do you leave with your winnings or do you play "just one more hand"?

Because of the volatility of currency it is near impossible to pick a peak so you should switch when you are comfortable with your gain, or worried about your loss.

With foreign currency movements, you must take your profits and minimise your losses. The face value interest savings are not enough.

If you do not take advantage of your opportunity, what is the point in seeking it, as it would not warrant the risk?.

You should also be reminded that you will not be able to continue with your multi currency facility when you return to Australia. You will be required to switch back to Australian dollars and may be forced to refinance.

I am not a currency specialist, nor do I want to even remotely make comment on where currency levels can move to.

All I can do is bring to your attention the real issues with foreign currency loans and remind you of the key rules that can provide you with some success and safety.

In summary they are :

- Australian Dollar lending offers no risk or opportunity,
- Multi Currency Loans must have the ability to switch quickly and cost effectively,
- Always borrow in the currency most likely to weaken,
- Be fully aware of the volatility of currencies and monitor the movements very closely,
- Take your profits and reduce your losses at appropriate times when the movement cycle is at or near its end,
- Don't get too greedy,
- Seek out as much information and quality professional advice on currency matters as you can,
- When there is relative stability in the currency, consider the merit of staying in the currency of least face value interest rate.
- When in doubt, always borrow in Australian dollars.

The opportunities offered by multi currency lending are real and achievable as long as you carefully monitor your position and are willing to accept the risks and potential downside.

The table we looked at in the beginning of this chapter mimics one of our unique Property Investors Tools on the ***aussieproperty.com*** website, The Foreign Currency Assessor.

This tool has been designed to allow you to make a full and proper assessment of the risk or benefit of Multi Currency lending.

You can quickly enter your expectations on each rollover date as to where you believe the currency will move to and it will properly calculate the true cost of borrowing, compare to the Australian dollar alternative and give a recommendation based on your projections.

This is a unique tool that we developed to help you minimise risk and maximise opportunity, so I hope it is of benefit to you and I would strongly recommend you take advantage of it if you are currently in or considering a Multi Currency Loan.

I have a fairly conservative nature so I am more in favour of Australian dollar lending unless the opportunity is very obvious.

As mentioned, investing quite often has enough risks without bringing in new ones that you do not need.

20. Returning To Australia

Let's look forward now. Hopefully you found this book fairly early in your expatriate life, and have put your plan into action.

As such you have a reasonable property portfolio and some other investments to give you a high quality lifestyle with great opportunity to reduce your income tax burden.

Now that you are returning to Australia, there are some important matters that you need to consider.

Value All Assets

You may recall that when you left Australia, the tax law deemed that you sold all your non-property assets. In the same way, upon your return you are deemed to acquire all assets when you arrive.

This is because you are now a resident of Australia for tax purposes as you will be living there permanently from now on.

That means you are now taxed on all worldwide income and capital gains.

The tax system will require you to conduct a valuation on all assets to establish the taxing point. Fortunately all gains you may have made on the asset prior to your return will be tax free, as will any built up cash or savings.

Your Australian properties will not be affected by this process, as they have remained taxable even whilst you were a non resident taxpayer.

For assets such as shares and unit trusts the valuation is as simple as getting the last market price prior to your date of arrival.

For other assets such as non Australian property or other assets, a sworn valuation will need to be obtained from an appropriately qualified person.

If the assets are sold after your return to Australia, then the taxable capital gain will be the difference between the sale price and the valuation upon return. The actual profit made will not be considered.

Whatever you have accumulated while living abroad will not be taxed on your return to Australia, but the future profits may be.

If you sold the assets 12 months after your return, then you will also be entitled to the 50% discount before any Capital gains tax is levied.

Make sure you do undertake your valuations so you do not expose yourself to the tax office making its own valuation, which may result in a higher taxable profit in sale.

Tax Losses Now Available

Whatever level of tax credits you have built up through your tax planning are now available to you.

These can offset any Australian taxable income including salary or investment income. It may also be used to offset any taxable capital gains.

Losses cannot be used on an "as required" basis. They are simply used in order of necessity. When you have income it will progressively reduce your tax credits until they are fully extinguished.

If you are to resume a salary position, you will have the choice to have the tax savings as an annual refund or a regular reduction in each pay period.

This will give you an opportunity to readjust to the Australian tax system gradually while you settle back into Australia.

Now you will experience the true value of your planning as it is no longer a future benefit, it is a today benefit.

Depending on your circumstances, these losses can be prolonged for a long time, particularly if you are returning for retirement.

Remember, you were in control as to how much you built up during your time as an expatriate, so I hope you looked after yourself.

Cash for My Castle

Now is the time to pay cash for your home or pay off the mortgage, if you had been fortunate enough to have found it while you were overseas.

The day to pay the residence out is on the day you actually move in and are sure it will be your long-term residence. If there is any doubt at all you should delay the payout of the mortgage in case the cash is required to acquire another residence.

Most Australian banks offer Offset Accounts where money can be deposited and linked to the loan. Whatever the balance on deposit will earn no interest, however the equivalent sum on your loan will be interest free.

This has the same affect as paying off the loan as the interest is reduced, but allows access to your cash to be maintained to apply to the future residence, while maintaining the loan on the existing property so it can be claimed when the property is rented out once again.

Not only should you clear the home loan, but also should pay cash for any other private items you want to purchase. This includes "toys" like boats or cars.

This is because you do not want any private debt when living in Australia. This is not always possible but should be your goal in your savings plans while abroad.

Private debt is non-tax deductible and therefore far more expensive on a pre-tax basis.

The key to survival in Australia from a tax perspective is to keep private expenses down to a minimum. Your home mortgage and private loan repayments are normally the single biggest private cost, and the only one you have the power to eliminate.

This is further highlighted by the fact that your residence is almost the only Capital Gains Tax free asset in Australia. So you should seek the best growth prospects with the lowest interest cost.

The effort that you have put in while you were overseas will now be very rewarding if you can in fact return to Australia with no private debt.

Assess the Need to Retain Negative Gearing

Private debt is the enemy of all Australian taxpayers. Alternatively, investment debt is the friend.

In this book we have worked through the financial and tax advantages of using borrowed funds to acquire quality investment property.

This system works well regardless of whether or not you live in Australia.

When you return to Australia, you will need to assess how to handle the investment property loans that you have taken out whilst abroad.

This will be greatly influenced by your circumstances.

If you are returning to a high salary position, it may well be that you should maintain the loans on the properties that continue to be rented out. This will allow you to continue to build tax losses which can then be offset against your salary on a yearly basis.

Depending on what level of depreciation allowance you have, you may well find that the annual cash holding cost is fully covered by the annual tax saving on the property.

This may well mean that keeping the loans is most tax effective on an ongoing basis.

Alternatively, if you are returning to Australia for retirement and have sufficient cash to clear the loans, it may well be best to pay off the loans and receive the rental as an income stream to fund your lifestyle.

Even if you simply reduce the loans to a level where the rents cover the mortgage repayments, this may be preferential to full repayment as it can ensure a tax-free retirement.

At this early stage it is impossible to predict, as so much depends on your savings built up and career options.

Safe to say that the more you save whilst away, the better the options will be when you return.

Superannuation

Any superannuation or pension funds that you have built up whilst overseas also need to be considered.

When you return to Australia, you have six months to decide as to what to do with your foreign superannuation before it comes under the tax regulations in Australia.

As such you need to decide whether or not to cash out or transfer the benefits.

Normally, if you come from a low tax regime it is better to cash out and pay the lower tax levels in that country before or upon your return to Australia.

If the tax regime you are leaving is also quite expensive then rolling it into an Australian fund may prove the best option.

A lot will also depend on the cost effectiveness of each choice. There may be high surrender costs that need to be considered.

Proper thought in collaboration with your financial planner is recommended.

There are also some very attractive incentives currently available for voluntary contributions to an Australian Superannuation Fund that should be investigated with your advisors.

Australian Tax Structures

When you return to Australia, it may well be beneficial to investigate the use of tax advantaged structures such as Companies or Family Trusts as they can offer some advantages to the Australian resident in controlling income and capital gains tax.

As this is a very individual matter, it is not appropriate to go to great lengths in this book, but it is something you should bear in mind.

These structures should not be established until you are confirmed to return to Australia and you need to be mindful when considering transferring assets into them as it may have tax implications (both in Australia and abroad), stamp duty, transfer costs and other legal issues.

You should always seek professional advice prior to any decisions in this regard.

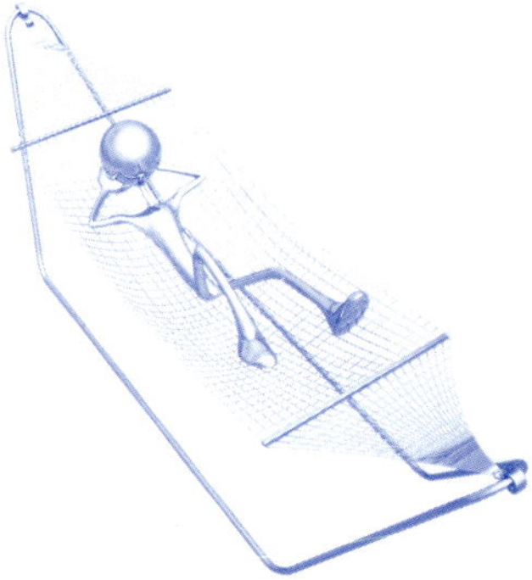

If you address these issues and keep your private costs to a minimum, it is indeed possible to maintain a very low tax life when you return to Australia, built firmly on the foundations of the planning undertaken whilst you lived as an expatriate.

21. Don't Lose Sight Of Your Goals

I hope I have given you reason to assess how you look at your savings programs and think about an eventual life back in Australia.

Starting this plan is as easy as thinking how much you may need to purchase your eventual home when you return to Australia, then working out how much you can save towards that goal.

Acquiring quality Australian property along the way is essential not only as a build up of your wealth but also to ensure you keep pace with the Australian market so you are not outpriced when you return.

I am sure you had specific reasons for coming abroad in the first place.

Your future is always more valuable than today, the sooner you realize that the better.

I am asking you to clearly identify those reasons, your future desires and time frames involved so that you can achieve an incredible financially sound life back in Australia one day.

Make sure you add to your list of goals these two very important ones:

- **Have sufficient liquid assets to pay cash for, or payout, your home.**
- **Build up enough tax credits to reduce the impact of tax on your return to Australia.**

The rest of your personal goals are up to you.

This system works regardless of your earning power, no matter if you have one property or one hundred.

It is very simple to safely and legitimately plan for any circumstance no matter if you have thousands or millions of dollars you have to invest and protect against a future Australian tax burden.

If you need help, there is always an ATS expert not far away (we are only a click away at *www.smats.net*) and will be happy to help to customise a plan especially for you.

22. Get To It

You have an opportunity to make a permanent difference in your future financial life.

The level of benefit you achieve whilst overseas is solely dependant on you. Hopefully this book has provided you with the ability to make informed and positive decisions.

Time is your only enemy, it disappears very quickly and never gives you a second chance.

In summary there are some key issues to remember as an expatriate.

On leaving:

- Determine whether to pay or defer Capital Gains Tax on non-property taxable assets.
- Restructure your Superannuation benefits to comply with regulations.
- Determine depreciation levels on family home if rented out.

Whilst you're overseas:

- Reduce all debt that is **NOT** related to income producing Australian property.
- Actively seek to invest in quality Australian property and utilise the tax benefits of borrowing and depreciation allowances.
- Build up the maximum tax losses through negative gearing during the period you are overseas.
- Commit to a real and achievable savings and investment plan for the benefit of your future.
- Save as much as possible utilising prudent investment mediums such as cash deposits, direct shares and public unit trusts.
- Build up liquid investments that can be cashed to acquire or pay off your future residence.

With all things, you need to constantly monitor and adapt your plans to fit your ever-changing goals and circumstances. An annual review should be conducted as a minimum.

Following these general principals can ensure that you return to Australia with a substantial portion of your earnings intact and a sizable buffer against income and capital gains tax on your future earnings.

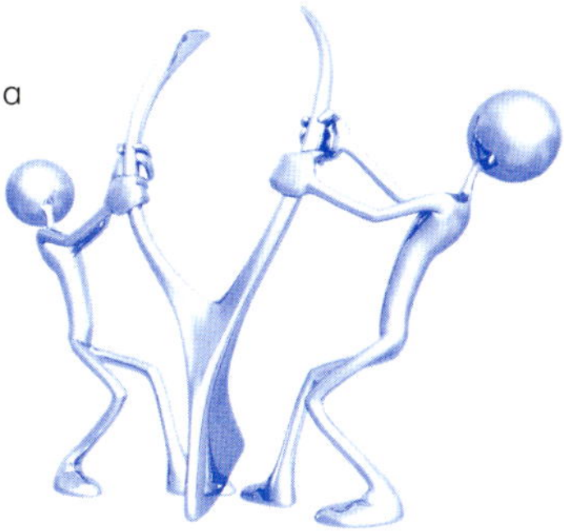

Good luck, you deserve it!

Dedications

I would like to thank all the expatriates that I have spoken to for prompting me to write this book, your frustrations in finding quality Australian Tax information was my inspiration.

No longer will you wonder in the wilderness, and may your lives be richer for the knowledge gained.

To all those that acquired the 1st Edition and provided me with valuable feedback allowing me to improve and enhance the 2nd Edition.

With love and thanks, I dedicate this book to:

Helen who has changed my life so positively,
Ravin my Singapore rock,
Rod who watches over me and helps me tune my guitar, and
Dr Tham and Sheena, whose support let me follow my dream.

A special thanks to my countless clients and friends that have helped me with their tales and actions, and to Janet for helping fate lead me to Asia.